TWIN SENSE

TWIN SENSE

A SANITY-SAVING GUIDE TO RAISING TWINS—
FROM PREGNANCY THROUGH THE FIRST YEAR

Dagmara Scalise

AMACOM

American Management Association

New York • Atlanta • Brussels • Chicago • Mexico City • San Francisco
Shanghai • Tokyo • Toronto • Washington, D.C.

Special discounts on bulk quantities of AMACOM books are available to corporations, professional associations, and other organizations. For details, contact Special Sales Department, AMACOM, a division of American Management Association, 1601 Broadway, New York, NY 10019.
Tel: 212-903-8316. Fax: 212-903-8083.
E-mail: specialsls@amanet.org
Website: www.amacombooks.org/go/specialsales
To view all AMACOM titles go to: www.amacombooks.org

This publication is designed to provide accurate and authoritative information in regard to the subject matter covered. It is sold with the understanding that the publisher is not engaged in rendering legal, accounting, or other professional service. If legal advice or other expert assistance is required, the services of a competent professional person should be sought.

Various names used by companies to distinguish their software and other products can be claimed as trademarks. AMACOM uses such names throughout this book for editorial purposes only, with no intention of trademark violation. All such software or product names are in initial capital letters or ALL CAPITAL letters. Individual companies should be contacted for complete information regarding trademarks and registration. A list of trademarked terms appearing in this book can be found on page vi.

Library of Congress Cataloging-in-Publication Data

Scalise, Dagmara.
    Twin sense : a sanity-saving guide to raising twins—from pregnancy through the first year / Dagmara Scalise.
        p. cm.
    Includes index.
    ISBN 978-0-8144-1066-0 (pbk.)
    1. Twins. 2. Infants—Care. 3. Infants—Development. 4. Multiple pregnancy. 5. Multiple birth. I. Title.

    HQ777.35.S32 2009
    649'.144—dc22   2008016649

Printing number

10   9   8   7   6   5   4   3   2   1

To Hope, Julian, and Katrina,
who made all the work worthwhile.

Following is a list of trademarked terms appearing in *Twin Sense*:

Advil
Babies "R" Us
Baby Trend
Baby's Away
Baggie
Barbie
BedBugz
Beech-Nut
Belly Belt
BOB Gear
BOB Revolution
Boppy
Boudreaux's Butt Paste
Britax
Cabbage Patch
Carnation
Cheerios
Cocteau Twins
Color Wonder
Costco
Craigslist
Crayola
Crock-Pot
Desitin Creamy
Diaper Champ
Disney World
Dora the Explorer
Double Blessings
Drypers
DuoGlider
eBay
Evenflo
Exersaucer
EZ-2-Nurse
First Year
Fisher-Price
Free Spirit Publishing
Guardian Angel
Go-Go Babyz
gogo Kidz

Graco
Gymini
HarperCollins
Healthtex
Home Depot
Huggies
Ikea
IlluStory
ING Direct
ING Orange Savings
 Account
International Board of
 Lactation Consultant
 Examiners
International Lactation
 Consultant Association
J. L. Childress Co., Inc.
KFC
Kimberly-Clark
Kirkland Signature
La Leche League
LeapPad
Leapster
Lillian Vernon
Mac
MacLaren
Mad Libs
Magic Eraser
Magna Doodle
Make It About Me!
McDonald's
Meijer
Minnesota Twins
Mountain Buggy
Mylicon
Nana Enterprises
Nestle
Netflix
One Step Ahead

Orange Account
Pack 'n Play
Peapod
PhotoWorks
Plexiglas
Podee
Pottery Barn Kids
Q-Tip
SafeSeat
Safety 1st
Sam's Club
Sharebuilder
Shutterfly
Sippy Cup
Sittercity.com
Snap-N-Go
SnugRide
Step2
Target
The First Years
The Right Start
The Step2 Company
The Traveling Baby
 Company
Thermos
Tiny Love
TiVo
ToddlerCoddler
Tripadvisor
Triple Paste
Tylenol
Vacationrentals.com
Valco
Velcro
Weleda
Whole Foods
Wiffle
Wii
Ziploc

Contents

🌹 PART TWO: MANAGING THE BASICS 🌹

❦ PART THREE: LEAVING THE HOUSE ❧

11: Making Errands Possible 107

12: Preparing, Packing, and Bundling Your Twins for a Car Ride 116

🌶 PART FOUR: LIFE AFTER BABYHOOD 🌶

15: Keeping the Peace 151

16: Baby-Proofing Your Home 161

Acknowledgments

I'd like to thank my editor, Bob Nirkind, for his invaluable help with the book, and my agent, Gina Panettieri, who saw its potential when it was merely an idea. I'd also like to thank all the parents of twins whose advice, information, and strategies I used in real life and included in the book. Although there are far too many people to thank by name, I'd specifically like to acknowledge Hilary Nielsen, Melissa and Gunnar Maehl, Nicole Marks, and Vicky Masciopinto for their excellent tips; Jennifer Hornberger, Laura Engel, Denise Joiner, and Jane Jeffries for putting me in touch with so many parents of twins; my husband Steve for his support, both during the course of writing the book and during the first few months when our twins were babies; and my mom, Krystyna, for her tremendous help in caring for our children.

TWIN SENSE

Introduction

Welcome to the club. Now that you or someone you love is having twins, you will have to relearn everything you thought you knew about parenting. Ignore that old saying about parenting twins being twice as hard. Those who have been there know the truth: Parenting twins is exponentially harder. Twin babies demand more love, more care, more patience, and more resourcefulness—lots more—and you, the parent, will be more stressed and less prepared than if you were having a single baby.

The information in *Twin Sense* is your secret weapon. It's the collected wisdom of other parents of twins—their best advice and tips—and it'll help you deal with all the things that aren't in most books, the things you usually have to learn by doing: what to buy and what to borrow, how to put one baby to sleep without waking the other, how to hold and feed both babies at once, how to go to the grocery store with two babies in tow, and how to travel with your babies and thirteen pieces of luggage. And because the book is organized by task, you'll be able to flip through the pages to find a solution to the problem you're having *now,* as well as get ideas on how to prevent similar problems in the future.

In my research for this book, I learned that my experience in becoming a parent of twins was pretty typical: There was panic and planning, followed by the sobering shock of reality. The day my doctor told me I was pregnant with twins I didn't bat an eye. "Twins? Great," I said. It wasn't until the next day that the panic and horror set in. How could I take care of twins? Having had one baby, I knew how hard it could be. There was no way I could handle twins. I wasn't sure if I was going to cry, throw up, or both. And then the feeling passed. I had a mission: to learn whatever I could about parenting twins. For months I read everything I could get my hands on and talked to everyone I could think of, and then lectured my husband and my mother. I'd be ready when the moment came. And you know what? I was still rocked by the enormity of it all.

That's what it's like for most new parents of twins. They're simply unprepared for what's in store for them. It's only after the babies are born and the parents have lived through a few weeks of sleepless nights, endless feedings, and total exhaustion that they begin to get their bearings. But it doesn't have to be that hard.

As I look back at my own experience, I realize now that for all my preparation, I didn't have the right information. I didn't know the true secrets of parenting twins—the strategies and advice that make the difference between feeling like a success and feeling like a failure as a parent. Thousands of other parents had been through this experience already, but I didn't know what they knew. If only I had been able to tap into that vast body of knowledge. The question was, how?

As it turns out, it involved a lot of legwork and research. But if you go to any playground, store, or other place where people with twins congregate, they'll happily share tips on where to get the best baby products, how to bathe both babies while entertaining a toddler, and how to go on vacation with twins without going nuts. I've spoken to scores of these parents and gathered their advice for you on the following pages. Life with twins is possible and—big drumroll—can be fun.

PART ONE

PREPARING FOR TWINS

How Different Can Having Twins Be?

You've just learned the news. You're having twins! You're euphoric, exhilarated, and rightly so. Learning that you will have twins is exciting. Although a lot of people do seem to be having twins these days, it's still a pretty exclusive club, and you will be guaranteed to get extra attention from family, friends, and even total strangers from the moment you tell the world.

So how different can having twins be? After all, it's not like it's rocket science—they're just babies. And if you've already had one child or two, then you've got some experience. Conventional wisdom suggests that having twins is twice as hard as having a single baby. You basically have to do everything twice and buy twice as much of everything. But the truth is, a twin pregnancy is unlike a singleton pregnancy from the get-go, and parenting twins demands more time, energy, and resources than parents of singletons or any new parent can imagine. It's not just that you have two babies; it's that those two babies make some of life's most basic tasks, things you now take for granted, like getting dressed or taking care of errands, a virtual Olympian challenge! And the challenges just keep coming as your twins grow.

Things are different from the start. During pregnancy, expect more doctors' visits and more tests. During delivery, expect far more people in the delivery room. Also, say good-bye to your money, because twins are definitely more expensive, from the food you feed them to the kind of car you buy for transporting your new, larger family. And say good-bye to your free time, because caring for twins is hard, physical work and you will have far less time for yourself, or for anything beyond the babies, in the initial few months. In addition, you may have to deal with your babies' special health issues, and you may have special health issues of your own. That's why knowledge and preparation are key.

Financial Considerations
✓ Accept that having twins will be more expensive.
✓ Borrow what you need.
✓ Save early, save often.
✓ Explore flexible spending accounts or health savings accounts.
✓ Make big purchases with your twins in mind.

During Pregnancy
✓ Prepare for more visits to the doctor.
✓ Make special arrangements to accommodate visits to the doctor.
✓ Expect more medical tests.
✓ Think about prenatal testing.
✓ Take specialized pregnancy classes for twins or multiples.
✓ Get informed about preemies.
✓ Anticipate bed rest.
✓ Fight boredom.
✓ Get Internet service; go wireless.

In the Hospital
✓ Expect to be wheeled into an operating room.
✓ Expect a crowd.
✓ Prepare to bottle-feed.

At Home Afterward
✓ Arrange for help.
✓ Stock up on necessities.
✓ Say good-bye to free time for the time being.
✓ Say yes to babysitting.

Special Challenges: C-Section Complications
✓ Don't be too hard on yourself.
✓ Use photos or video to keep involved and share special moments.

Special Challenges: Caring for Preemies
✓ Arm yourself with knowledge.
✓ Communicate with hospital staff.
✓ Be persistent.
✓ Find an advocate.

✓ Get a night nurse.

✓ Seek emotional support.

FINANCIAL CONSIDERATIONS

It's no secret that having kids is expensive, but having twins means you have an even greater need to plan for the financial challenges ahead.

Accept That Having Twins Will Be More Expensive

From the moment you become pregnant, a twin pregnancy seems to require more money. You grow out of your maternity clothes at warp speed and have to buy more and more clothes just to keep your belly covered. If your health insurance requires co-pays, you will have to pay for more doctors' visits and tests. And, of course, you need beds, mattresses, bassinets, car seats, diaper bags, and the like, in plural!

Borrow What You Need

Sure, it's nice to have new things, especially if these are your first babies. But twins require so much stuff, and so much of it is immediately outgrown, that borrowing from friends and family is a smart option.

Save Early, Save Often

Save early, save often means buying things like diapers and wipes in bulk. It also means saving for your babies. Investigate savings options for your twins, such as higher-interest savings accounts like ING's Orange Account, or purchase low-cost stocks through companies like Sharebuilder.com.

Explore Flexible Spending Accounts or Health Savings Accounts

Ideally, you set up and use flexible spending or health savings accounts for your medical expenses before you get pregnant, but even if you set them up while you're pregnant or when your twins are born, you will offset medical expenses by tapping into pretax funds.

Make Big Purchases with Your Twins in Mind

A perfect example of a big purchase you'll need to make in advance of your twins' arrival is the family car. A car that is fine for a family with one child, or even one older child and a baby, is not really great for a family with twins. Even if you can fit your twins into the backseat of your midsize car, once you think about all the gear you'll have to carry for the next several years, such as strollers, diaper bags, baby carriers, clothes, and wagons, many "roomy" cars become as cramped as matchboxes. Plan accordingly.

DURING PREGNANCY

Twin pregnancies differ from singleton pregnancies from the first doctor's visit—expect more medical management, more time spent at appointments, and more tests.

Prepare for More Visits to the Doctor

It's a given that pregnancy-related doctors' visits take up a lot of time, especially if you have to factor in a long commute. In a typical singleton pregnancy, a woman may see her obstetrician roughly twelve to fifteen times before delivering her baby. For the first six months, she will see her doctor once a month, then twice a month for months seven and eight, and finally once a week for the last two to four weeks of her pregnancy. Contrast that with a woman who is pregnant with twins. While your initial visit may take place in the same time frame as a woman carrying a single baby (anywhere from the week you find out you are pregnant to several weeks out, depending on your practice), as soon as your doctor confirms you are having twins, you are likely to immediately start seeing the doctor twice a month, and then once a week from week 32 on. That's roughly 30 percent more doctor visits for moms of twins.

Make Special Arrangements to Accommodate Visits to the Doctor

Be sure to arrange for extra time off from your employer or arrange for childcare to accommodate your schedule. And remember you will have to find time in your schedule to work in extra medical tests as well!

Expect More Medical Tests

If you became pregnant with medical help, then you are likely to know that you're having twins early on. If your pregnancy is a surprise, it may take some time and several visits to the doctor to learn that you're having twins. Either way, women who are pregnant with multiples are subject to more tests, including earlier and more frequent ultrasounds (often at every single visit); fetal heart monitoring as the pregnancy progresses; and, frequently, genetic testing.

Think About Prenatal Testing

Women of advanced maternal age, defined in this context as thirty-five or older, are generally offered the option of genetic testing to screen their babies for Down syndrome or other genetic problems. Older women typically undergo amniocentesis between sixteen and twenty weeks. However, if you are carrying twins, your doctor may prefer that you undergo a test called *chorionic villus sampling*, or CVS. Unlike amniocentesis, this test is done much earlier, generally between eleven and twelve weeks of pregnancy. (Many testing centers will not do the test after week 12.) So if you are interested in prenatal screening or anticipate that your doctor will recommend it, talk to your doctor early during your pregnancy, so you are fully prepared to make the right decision for you.

Take Specialized Pregnancy Classes for Twins or Multiples
Specialized pregnancy classes are great at familiarizing you with the delivery and hospital experience, and they are especially targeted to parents of multiples. For example, the classes often will show a film of a twin delivery and include a tour of the neonatal intensive care unit (NICU). Be sure to schedule the class early on in your pregnancy, as early as sixteen weeks. In many cases, women who plan to take the classes later miss out because they end up on bed rest.

Get Informed About Preemies
If your twins are born prior to thirty-six weeks, there's a good chance they will be admitted to the NICU. They may even stay in the hospital after you're discharged. This is simultaneously a joyful yet stressful time. On the one hand, your long-awaited babies are here. On the other, their health is at issue and you may have to leave them. Help yourself manage this emotional firestorm by preparing ahead of time: Read, ask questions, and familiarize yourself with what happens if your babies are born prematurely, so that you can be assured that you are doing what is best for them.

Anticipate Bed Rest
Many women carrying twins (and other multiples) find that they are forced to go on bed rest, even if they thought they were in optimal health. It's just a reality: Twin pregnancies carry more risks for the babies and for the mother-to-be. Twins have a higher likelihood of being born prematurely (before thirty-six weeks for twins is considered premature). To prevent this, many women are put on bed rest by their physicians, either as a precaution or in response to preterm labor. Even if your babies are in ideal health, there are numerous sources of physical and emotional stress—such as having other children to care for, working full-time, or caring for family members—that can take a toll on your body and have a negative impact on your pregnancy. Your doctor may put you on bed rest for a short two-week period at the end

of your pregnancy, or you may find that you have to be on bed rest for three or four months of your pregnancy. It's best to prepare yourself emotionally for this challenge ahead of time (when you first learn you're pregnant or in the first trimester) and plan on how you might handle several weeks or months when your activities are severely restricted.

Anticipating bed rest is one thing, but planning for extended bed rest is another. If you have the luxury of working for a large employer who offers sick time and medical leave, then do your utmost to stay on bed rest after your babies' birth. But many women may feel they are forced to work, even if they have a medical reason not to. It could be for financial reasons or because a small company depends on them to keep the business going. (Companies that employ fewer than fifty people are not required to abide by the Family and Medical Leave Act, which grants eligible employees twelve weeks of unpaid time off for the birth of a child.) How can you work and still abide by your doctor's orders? Talk with your employer in advance about its expectations. Check to see if telecommuting is an option; perhaps arrange a step-down schedule in which you initially work from home and gradually do less and less work while on bed rest. The key is to plan to be out of work.

Fight Boredom

The blunt truth is that bed rest is boring. There's only so much television you can watch and only so many books or magazines you can read. Plan projects that can be done while reclining—for example, creating and addressing baby announcements, crafts like knitting and crocheting, organizing those photos you've been meaning to—but do not expect you will get anything done that requires standing, sitting for extended periods, bending, or walking. That includes cooking and working on the babies' room. Forget about it and lay back down.

Get Internet Service; Go Wireless

Go online, check out the twins forums, and read about women going through the same experience you are. Learn about caring for preemies. Update your blog. Having access to the Internet will make you feel more connected to the world while you're on bed rest; having a wireless Internet connection gives you options for "exploring" other areas of your house besides the bedroom.

IN THE HOSPITAL

The high-risk nature of a twin pregnancy means your delivery experience will be a lot more "medical" than if you were delivering a single baby.

Expect to Be Wheeled into an Operating Room

Whether you have a C-section or deliver your babies vaginally, your delivery is considered high-risk and you will be taken to an operating room. And unlike the homey environment many hospitals create in their maternity wards, sterile operating rooms are not exactly welcoming. The lights, equipment, and cold temperatures in an operating room make it easy to feel overwhelmed and frightened. However, just knowing what you can expect when you deliver may calm your nerves, as can talking to your doctor or even a nurse on staff about the environment and the delivery process.

Expect a Crowd

A woman pregnant with a single baby may have her doctor, a nurse, and her spouse in the delivery room. She may even have her mom, sister, or best friend there. This is not the case for women pregnant with twins. Two babies means that you will have entire medical teams for each baby in the delivery room. It's not uncommon for there to be as many as ten people in the room, plus you and your spouse. That doesn't leave much room for anyone else you may have wanted to be there. And regardless, many hospitals have policies that prohibit anyone besides your spouse from being in the room.

Prepare to Bottle-Feed

If you're committed to breast-feeding, you may be surprised if the hospital staff asks you to immediately bottle-feed your twins. I know I was. Twins, especially preemies, tend to have lower birth weights, and the primary goal of the nursing staff is to make sure your babies are gaining weight appropriately. Although you may be able to breast-feed in addition to using bottles, in the initial hours after birth you're quite likely to be giving your twins formula.

AT HOME AFTERWARD

The enormous impact of having two babies will become evident as soon as you leave the hospital and are on your own. Preparation is key.

Arrange for Help

Help can mean your husband, your mom, a friend, or a night nurse. As a new mom with twins you will absolutely need resources, especially if you deliver your babies by C-section and cannot walk because of complications. Even if you have an uneventful pregnancy and an easy delivery, until you get your bearings, taking care of two babies really does require two adults.

Stock Up on Necessities

Two babies mean you will need extra diapers, extra wipes, extra clothes, extra everything. (Chapter 4 covers what you need for twins.) Mentally prepare yourself to hunker down for a while and stock up on necessities for the babies and for yourselves.

Say Good-Bye to Free Time for the Time Being

Twins require a lot of work, even for people who are used to doing it all. They take strength, stamina, and savvy scheduling. Moms who plan on having friends and family visit should reassess their expectations as to how their homes will look or feel. Your house will be messy and your clothes will be stained when people come to visit. It's likely that you will not even have much time to talk to your guests while they're visiting, given that your babies will require plenty of attention and care. Better yet, put those guests to work and get some sleep yourself.

Say Yes to Babysitting

Well-meaning friends and family will probably offer to babysit. Take them up on the offer. Then don't do laundry or clean the house. Instead go to sleep. Or get out of the house. Do something for your own sanity.

SPECIAL CHALLENGES: C-SECTION COMPLICATIONS

If you find your delivery did not go as you envisioned and you end up with complications, take steps to bond with your babies, even if you're bedridden.

Don't Be Too Hard on Yourself

It's not uncommon for women with twins to deliver their babies by C-section. In many cases, a vaginal delivery is simply not possible, either because the babies are not positioned correctly or because there are other medical/health issues involved. But although C-sections may be the safest way to deliver the babies, you can be down for the count after giving birth and your partner will have to be the primary caregiver in the days after you deliver. Don't beat yourself up. Just concentrate on getting better and rest up for when it's your turn to care for the babies.

Use Photos or Video to Keep Involved and Share Special Moments

If you are bedridden after your C-section or hospitalized with complications, you may feel as though you've missed out on the special moments in the twins' first days or weeks. Have your spouse or partner take photos or videos of the babies yawning or wearing their first outfits, so you can enjoy them once you feel better.

SPECIAL CHALLENGES: CARING FOR PREEMIES

If your babies are born prematurely, there are strategies to help you manage the added stress of worrying about their health and well-being.

Arm Yourself with Knowledge

Premature births occur in more than 60 percent of twin pregnancies, which is defined as delivery before thirty-seven weeks. Know what challenges your twins might face.

Communicate with Hospital Staff

When your babies are in the hospital, it's a relief to know that someone with experience is caring for them. But if you have to leave while your babies stay, it's easy to feel disconnected. Call the nurses, ask questions about what they're doing, and take notes on anything you don't understand. And, before leaving the hospital, make sure you take down the names of everyone on the nursing staff, so you know whom to contact.

Be Persistent

Don't let a busy hospital staff member deter you from doing what's best for your babies. Persist in asking questions and seeking information.

Find an Advocate

Parents of preemies may be too overwhelmed by the immediate needs of their babies and by their own emotions to ask questions and get information about their babies. Find a friend or a family member to step in and ask for you. This person brings the advantage of being more objective and clear-headed than you may be capable of being at this time and can help you navigate the healthcare system—the doctors, nurses, and specialists—when you need help the most.

Get a Night Nurse

Preemies can have a lot of issues, and if you're feeling overwhelmed, then ease into things by getting a night nurse. Although hospital staff will show you how to care for your babies while you are in the hospital, your confidence can deflate once you get home. Having an experienced nurse to show you the ropes in your own environment will make a huge difference.

Seek Emotional Support

This is a time to try to talk to an experienced counselor or other people who have dealt with similar issues. Contact the hospital or your OB for suggestions on support groups, or speak with someone from your place of worship.

2

Getting Information and Support for Your First Year with Twins

The day you learn you're having twins is also the day that you realize how unprepared you are for your new responsibilities and how little you actually know about twins. Getting informed about what you will experience is probably the best thing you can do for yourself and for your babies. It will give you an awareness of the upcoming challenges, build confidence in your parenting skills, and teach you how to become intrepid in getting what you need.

But getting informed can be a daunting task. No one you know has twins; you don't know what questions to ask or what books to read; and a brief Internet search for "twins" pulls up millions of sites, with information that may or may not be credible. How and where do you start?

Where to Begin
✓ Figure out what you want to know and where you can get your answers.
✓ Write down your questions.

What to Keep in Mind
✓ Not all information about twins is pregnancy-related.
✓ Not everything you need to know has to be twin-specific.
✓ Start, and finish, getting informed early.
✓ Don't get obsessed.
✓ Keep the information you find in a binder.

Where to Go for Information

✓ Ask your doctor.

✓ Look beyond an MD.

✓ Ask your midwife.

✓ Consult with experts based on your needs.

✓ Build your parenting network.

✓ Join a moms' group, or start one.

✓ Take hospital-sponsored parenting classes.

✓ Take advantage of hospital-based support groups.

✓ Use the hospital library.

✓ Reach out to twins or multiples clubs.

✓ Check your local paper for baby fairs.

✓ Look for local parenting magazines.

✓ Visit a baby store.

✓ Get book recommendations.

✓ Think of the Internet as a trail of clues.

✓ Start a blog.

In the early stages of pregnancy everything twins-related seems ultra-important. Then, in the first year of parenting your twins, you are so overwhelmed with day-to-day activities and so tired in general that everything twins-related *is* ultra-important. But before you start an intense search for information, bear in mind that you have to know what you want to learn and you have to maintain your perspective, which isn't always easy, given the circumstances.

WHERE TO BEGIN

Trying to learn about twins, as well as about how to make the most of your parenting experience, can be daunting. Before you start seeking information, figure out *what* you want to know.

Figure Out What You Want to Know and Where You Can Get Your Answers

Do you want to know if you will have monozygotic (identical) or dizygotic (fraternal) twins? Are you interested in how multiple pregnancies differ from singleton pregnancies, or if you can expect to gain more weight with twins than with a single baby? Perhaps you are more interested in how twins will affect your life or how they interact with each other. Although all of these questions are twins-related, they are actually very different topics, and to answer them you will likely have to seek information from very different resources. So before you subject yourself to information overload, figure out what you want to know and where you can get your answers. You'll save yourself time and effort down the line.

Write Down Your Questions

Once you figure out what you want to know, write down your questions. In the process, you may discover that the three or four different questions you thought you had are all actually variations of the same question. Or, you may find that you actually have many more questions than you originally thought. Make sure, too, that your spouse or partner writes down his questions as well. You may find that what you're concerned about is not necessarily what he's concerned about.

WHAT TO KEEP IN MIND

As you begin to gather information, there are a few caveats to remember.

Not All Information About Twins Is Pregnancy-Related

There's a tendency for parents-to-be to focus on the here and now. They want to know how their babies are developing, how much they weigh, what positions they're in, and what sex they are. This is only natural. During pregnancy it's all about you (or your partner), because everything beyond pregnancy seems pretty far off. But as prospective parents, you and your partner will want to know how to actually take care of your babies once they're born. Give some thought to other information you're going to want to know—such as information having to do with health issues, breast-feeding, sharing, and bonding.

Not Everything You Need to Know Has to Be Twin-Specific

While there are many issues that are unique to twins and parents of twins, sometimes what you need to know is just related to general childcare and child health. Don't drive yourself crazy looking for information that is always twins-specific. Read general articles and extrapolate what you need. When your gut tells you that your experience with twins is very different from that described in articles targeted to singleton parents, pay attention to that feeling and delve further.

Start, and Finish, Getting Informed Early

There's a tendency for parents-to-be to think there's plenty of time to get things done, including getting ready to become parents of twins. Many put it off, thinking there'll be time later in the pregnancy. This is especially true if you have other children to take care of, if you work full-time, or both. You may simply feel you don't have the time right now. But the truth is, there's no extra time down the road, especially with twins, because a high percentage of them are born early. Learn what you can before you have your babies, because once you've given birth, you'll find you never have the time.

Don't Get Obsessed

There's such a thing as getting too much information. Too many parents (okay, in my experience, moms-to-be) focus on researching every aspect of their pregnancies and learning everything they can about twins. Although it's great to be informed, don't let your desire for information get in the way of other things, like getting some rest.

Keep the Information You Find in a Binder

Many women spend a good part of their pregnancies becoming mini-experts on twins. They consult with people; become members of parenting networks, clubs, and support groups; and read books and scour the Internet for information. However, once their babies are born, that information seems inexplicably lost and even the most basic question about twins elicits a blank stare or a round of head scratching. From personal experience, I can tell you there's almost nothing more incredibly frustrating than to have to re-create your initial search in order to find that great website with the stroller you thought about buying or to rack your brain to remember what book had those statistics on twin births. Rather than set yourself up for doing the same task twice, make it a habit to collect the information that you've discovered and keep it all in a binder that you can refer to in the future. If, in a year or two, you find you didn't really need it, you can toss the information then. But in the meantime, at least you'll have it available when your twins are small and you're looking for insights.

WHERE TO GO FOR INFORMATION

Okay, now that you know where to begin and what to keep in mind, where should you actually go to get the information you need? We can break it down into three general categories—people; institutions, organizations, clubs, fairs, and stores; and published and online information. Let's discuss all of them.

Ask Your Doctor

An obvious place to start is with your doctor, who can provide you with a lot of information on your twin pregnancy. But perhaps more important, your doctor can also put you in contact with other experts, as well as recommend books you should read. When I was pregnant, my doctor put me in touch with a nurse at a local hospital who was involved in a clinical study on multiple pregnancies. That nurse ended up being a valuable resource, someone who not only gave me information on a subject I hadn't thought about (how to prevent preterm labor in multiple pregnancies), but also a professional I saw regularly and knew I could approach with questions.

Look Beyond an MD

Your OB/GYN is a great resource for pregnancy-related issues but is probably not the best person to ask for questions about twin babies. Similarly, your pediatrician is a great resource for pediatric health issues but may not be an expert on twins or may not be an expert on your twins' actual medical conditions, if they were born prematurely. Start with your healthcare provider, but don't end there. You are the parents, so it is up to you to become the experts on your twins.

Ask Your Midwife

It's highly unlikely that women pregnant with multiples will have them delivered by a midwife; there are just too many medical risks involved and the medical management is too complicated. However, some women may see a midwife in the initial stages of a pregnancy, before they know they're having twins. A midwife can be a good resource, especially regarding issues like breast-feeding twins and alternative medical strategies.

Consult with Experts Based on Your Needs

There are nearly as many experts as there are twins-related issues: genetic consultants, lactation consultants, car seat experts (starting with the National Highway Traffic Safety Administration, or NHTSA, which provides car seat ratings), twins organizations, and so on. Don't expect any one resource to provide you with everything you need. Adopt a buffet mentality: Pick and choose among the options that suit your needs best at any given time.

Build Your Parenting Network

Most people understand the term *networking* as it pertains to business. The term refers to making contacts with people who can supply you with information about your field of interest, put you in touch with others in your field, or provide you with job leads. The same strategy works for parenting information. Though most of us automatically think to turn to family and friends with twins, far fewer of us think to go beyond this circle. But it's imperative to create contacts with others if you want practical advice and help. Simply put, other parents of twins can tell you things no one else can. How do you find them? You talk to people and tell them you're having twins. If they don't immediately mention that they know so-and-so has twins (most people mention it within the first couple of minutes of the conversation), ask if they know anyone. You'll be surprised at how many people you'll find and how many will be willing to talk to you.

Join a Moms' Group, or Start One

Whether it's once a week or once a month, meeting with other mothers of twins can be a lifeline in those first few months after the babies' births. Not only will these meetings give you an opportunity to actually get out of the house and speak with other adults, but in my experience other moms have the best tips and are the best listeners of all things baby. Join a multiples club, if possible. If not, join a regular moms' club, because then you'll find yourself getting the most sympathy. (You'll also develop a perverse sense of pride as you realize how much more work you have than the other moms!) If you don't know where to find a club, scan the bulletin board in your local library, the hospital where you gave birth, or in local baby stores and coffee shops. You'll be surprised at how many women in your situation are out there. If all else fails, start your own moms' group. Post flyers where new moms hang out—the library, your local park district, baby boutiques, area coffee shops, your pediatrician's office, or even your OB/GYN's office, or post an ad on Craigslist.

Take Hospital-Sponsored Parenting Classes

Most likely your local hospital offers specialized classes for parents of multiples where you can learn basics like swaddling and bathing your babies, as well as get a tour of the neonatal intensive care unit (NICU), which specializes in the care of sick or premature newborn infants. These classes will feature videos of twin births and cover topics unique to multiples. Given how informative they are, they should be mandatory for all parents-to-be, but especially for dads. There was a lot of eye-opening information in the classes my husband and I took, as well as a lot of commiserating with other people in our situation. Just remember to take these classes early, around weeks 16–20, if possible, when you're less likely to be put on bed rest.

Take Advantage of Hospital-Based Support Groups

Many hospitals, especially the larger ones in your community, will probably also offer staff-led support groups for new parents of multiples. These support groups are useful in that the people leading them are often healthcare professionals with expertise and personal experience with multiple births.

Use the Hospital Library

You may not know it, but there's a good chance your hospital has a library or research area with books, journals, and pamphlets of medical information, including material on multiple pregnancies. Hospital libraries are typically staffed by knowledgeable people who can help you with your research. They also have computers with access to scientific journals (most of which are available only to medical professionals or through subscriptions). If you are interested in specialized medical resources regarding pregnancy or twins, a hospital library should be on your list of destinations, especially since it will have already vetted the materials, which should give you added confidence that the information you find is medically credible. Just be sure to check the hours and/or days when the library is open and staffed.

Reach Out to Twins or Multiples Clubs

Many communities and regions have established twins or multiples clubs. These are organizations whose main focus it is to provide support networks and disseminate information on multiple births. Twins clubs are formalized versions of the kind of personal networks it takes most people a long time to build, so you can tap into some excellent resources right away, without any of the heavy lifting involved in building your own network. The drawback is that because they are local, their organizational structures vary; clubs may have different rules, and their locations or meeting times may not be convenient to you.

Check Your Local Paper for Baby Fairs

Many cities host "baby fairs," which are large events targeted to expectant and new parents that bring together vendors to showcase and sell their baby products. These events are usually weekend affairs held in convention centers, and they are typically advertised in local papers a month ahead of time. They are great resources for product information, including products that are twins-specific.

Look for Local Parenting Magazines

These free publications are usually advertiser-supported. They generally cover all sorts of parenting issues (not necessarily twins-specific), list local events, show twins clubs listings, and include pages and pages of ads from companies and businesses that cater to children and/or parents. Look for local parenting magazines in neighborhood stores as well as pediatrician offices or children's museums.

Visit a Baby Store

Some stores catering to expectant parents and parents of young children have promotional learning events where they bring in experts to teach parents basics, such as breast-feeding and baby massage. While the stores' strategy is, of course, to increase foot traffic, you can still gain valuable tips without cost, which just about fits the budget of most parents of twins.

Get Book Recommendations

Books on twins can be incredibly helpful (such as this one!), but not every book is right for every person. In the initial euphoria and panic that followed once I learned I was going to have twins, I bought four books on twins and pregnancy. Ultimately, though, I read only limited bits of two of the books and did not even get a chance to read either the third or the fourth. Not only was time an issue (as a working mom, I had none for myself, and that included reading about twins), but as I delved further I realized I didn't necessarily want all the information I thought I did. I ended up passing my books along to an acquaintance who was also pregnant with twins, along with my assessment of which books were the most helpful. Whenever possible, get recommendations from friends or go online and browse for some books with good reviews.

Think of the Internet as a Trail of Clues

The Internet is probably the most ubiquitous tool for gathering information on every topic under the sun, including twins. Despite its potential for usefulness, the Internet can also seem like a labyrinth, more confusing than helpful. If the online articles you find don't have the information you're looking for, search for clues on the websites you're already on. Watch for phrases that clearly indicate the focus you're curious or concerned about, or note the names of authors or experts who are knowledgeable in your area of interest. Then do related searches. Even seemingly unhelpful articles can often point you to other, more helpful resources.

To save yourself some time, do *not* do a search for "twins." Not only will you literally receive 50 million results, but the information will be completely unfiltered, so you'll get information on twins, twins pregnancies, the Minnesota Twins, the Olsen twins, the eighties band the Cocteau Twins, as well as links to blog pages, stores, and practically anything else you can imagine. Ask precise questions such as "How much weight should I expect to gain with my twin pregnancy?" or type in keywords such as "statistics twins birth weight" to narrow your search.

You want to avoid the information vortex. What typically happens is that you find one site that looks like it has great information, and because it gives you an idea about something else you'd like to know about, you do a related search. Alternatively, you do a search and methodically click on every link that was returned in your search. Before you know it, you've spent way more time than you wanted researching "just one thing" and you're now more confused than ever because you're on information overload. Give yourself a time limit and avoid the trap of checking out every link.

And keep in mind that not everything on the Internet is accurate or true. When conducting searches, pay attention to who is sponsoring the page, whether the source is credible, and if the site has any other agenda, such as selling products. Should you find that a lot of the same information appears on multiple sites, sometimes down to the exact wording, understand that is due to the fact that many sites purchase prewritten articles. When you find information that seems worthwhile, remember to put it in a larger context. You want to see whether any other sites provide alternative views or additional information.

Start a Blog

If you are web-savvy, consider starting a blog where you can share your news, updates, and concerns with family and friends. It's not only a convenient way to provide information, but it's also a great way to prompt people to contact you and provide you with information and support. You may also consider a blog if you want to create an online support group for other moms of twins, especially if you have friends or family in distant places.

3

Responding to Dumb or Probing Questions About Having Twins

As any pregnant woman will tell you, a baby belly is a magnet for comments. A woman who is pregnant with twins, though, is subject to even more questions, opinions, advice, and groping (yes, groping!) than a woman who is carrying a single baby. Our bellies are bigger, for one thing, so we're more noticeable. Strangers see us coming and feel *compelled* to say something.

In addition, when people hear you say you're carrying twins, their brains go on hiatus. They feel perfectly entitled to pose the most personal questions, make rude comments, and generally stick their feet in their mouths just because twins are less common than singleton babies. They're not necessarily trying to be offensive. They just feel emboldened to ask questions that probably shouldn't be asked, simply because they're naturally curious, attempting to be friendly, or trying to express their sympathy.

Your best strategy for responding to dumb or probing questions is to accept the fact that pregnancy sometimes demands a thick skin. Take things in stride when possible, set conversational limits when necessary, and develop effective comebacks for those moments when you just have to say something.

What follows are some of the questions and comments you're likely to hear, both during your pregnancy and after you have had your babies. I've personally heard the majority of them, as have most of the women I know with twins. During pregnancy, the comments tend to fall into a few standard categories: gestational origin, mom's weight or belly size, body issues, and remarks about your current and future lifestyle.

* Do twins run in your family?
* Did you use fertility treatments?

* Are you having twins because you're older?
* Oh, so your eggs are dropping at a faster rate. (I kid you not, someone actually said this to me!)
* You're only five months along! I wasn't as big as you at nine months!
* You're huge!
* Lady, you look like you're going to pop any minute.
* Just how many are in there?
* My God, I've never seen a belly so big.
* Can I call you doublewide?
* How much weight have you gained?
* Do you have stretch marks? (Or its close cousin: I'll bet you have stretch marks!)
* You're starting to get that pregnancy waddle.
* Were you trying for twins?
* Will you have to have a C-section?
* Are you going to breast-feed?
* Did you have sex twice?
* This is it, right?
* You're going to quit your job, aren't you?
* At least it's not triplets.
* Were you shocked when you found out?

After the birth of your babies, you're likely to hear another round of questions and comments regarding your babies' looks and behavior. You'll also get plenty of expressions of false sympathy or compassion (and sometimes genuine sympathy), as well as tales of twins or parents of twins the person knows and probing questions about how you are going to care for your babies and whether you are planning to have any more.

* Are they identical?
* Are they *really* twins? (Like you'd lie about it.)
* They look alike. Are they identical? (This one is priceless for boy-girl twins.)
* Do they act the same?
* Do they eat at the same time?
* Do they wake each other up?
* Do you feed them the same things?
* Oh, they look different. (Someone remarking this may sound disappointed.)
* Are their personalities the same?
* How do you tell them apart?

* Are they sleeping in the same bed?
* Which one is older?
* You sure have your hands full.
* I feel sorry for you.
* Thank God I'm not in your shoes.
* You poor thing!
* How do you manage?
* There's no way I'd want to be in your shoes.
* I hope you have help!
* Better you than me.
* I bet your husband was thrilled. (The questioner's voice is usually dripping with sarcasm.)
* You're lucky you got it over with at once.
* I wish I had twins.
* I've always wanted twins.
* So-and-so (my second cousin, my husband's niece, my mom's neighbor's daughter) has twins.
* Twins run in my family.
* Are you planning to have more?
* Are you breast-feeding?
* Did you plan to have twins?
* Now that you've got one of each, you're done, right?
* You've got double trouble.
* Did you have to go into labor twice?

A POSITIVE ATTITUDE IS YOUR BEST DEFENSE

Although at first you may be surprised at just how many remarks you're getting about your belly or your babies, it won't take long before you realize there's little you can do about it. A good attitude, a lot of patience, and a sense of humor will take the edge off when you hear how big you are for the tenth time in a week. What to do? Here are some suggestions.

Expect Comments

One of the positive things about our society is that pregnant women are still considered special and, consequently, receive a lot of attention from family, friends, and, like it or not, total strangers. So although you may feel like you want to be cocooned away with your developing babies during your pregnancy, the reality is that people will notice and say things, both positive and negative. Once you realize this fact, it won't come as such as shock the first time someone comments on your pregnancy.

Develop a Thick Skin

It seems that during pregnancy everyone wants to tell you two things: how awful her labor and delivery experience was (or that of his wife or sister, in the case of men) and how you should raise your children once they're born. Imagine being stuck on an elevator with someone who tells you her horror story of going into labor and the doctor not giving her an epidural, so she screamed bloody murder during her delivery. Or someone who tells you what an awful parent you will be if you dare to bottle-feed your children rather than breast-feed. Or how abusive it is to vaccinate babies when there is so much concern about mercury in vaccines and how everyone is brainwashed by the medical establishment. (I heard this comment with my first daughter when I stopped by a store, literally after just having had her vaccinated at the doctor's office!) The point here is, since you can't stop people from running off at the mouth and saying the most incredibly stupid, rude, or upsetting things, you're better off developing a thick skin so that their comments won't unduly hurt you.

Rely on Your Sense of Humor

The day I heard a homeless man say to me, "Lady, you look like you're going to pop any minute," I could have gotten upset or said something nasty. But where would it have gotten me? It would have just prolonged a conversation I didn't want to have in the first place. Instead, I just laughed it off and had a great story to tell my colleagues at work when I returned from my lunchtime errand. When you can, laugh it off.

Be Understanding

Pregnancy is one of those times when people want to express their interest in you or show their sympathy. It's important to understand that most people do not mean to be boorish; they just don't seem to realize how their comments are perceived. This is also true of people who comment on your babies. Seeing twins (or other multiples) is still a pretty infrequent occurrence for most folks, so it shouldn't be surprising that they don't know what moms of twins and moms-to-be want or don't want to hear. Take their often-bumbling efforts for what they are—an attempt to be sociable. Your effort to understand will pay off when you realize how much stress you save yourself.

Ignore Them If Possible

Like the boring uncle who insists on telling the same story over and over at every family gathering, or the next-door neighbor who relates every detail of her recent surgery as you're trying to take out the garbage, some people just beg to be ignored. When strangers offer their opinions on how much weight you've gained or how you choose to name, dress, or handle your babies, ignore them if possible. In many cases, responding to these people only gives them more opportunity to comment further. Pay no attention to them and chances are, once they've made their remarks, they'll go away.

Be Polite

It may seem unfair, but when people are rude to you, I'm advocating being polite. Politeness is really a social lubricant and it will let you get past the unwanted exchange smoothly. Plus, you'll feel better knowing that you were the bigger person and didn't stoop to the other person's level. In the long run, politeness saves you a lot of energy—no arguments and no obsessing over what you could have or should have said.

Enjoy Being the Center of Attention

When you first learn you're pregnant, especially when you're pregnant with twins, you want to tell the world! You tell your family and friends, call long-distance cousins, the whole gamut. Similarly, when your twins are born, you love how people just coo over your gorgeous babies. Sure, the novelty of all this attention wears off, but remember that pregnancy and the "cute baby" phase will end all too soon, and before you know it, most people will not give you a second glance. So enjoy the attention while it lasts.

WHEN A POSITIVE ATTITUDE JUST ISN'T GOOD ENOUGH

There will be times when you feel that having a sense of humor or being polite is just not appropriate or effective—for example, when interacting with the tiresome colleague who learns that you are bottle-feeding your twins and berates you for your choice, or the stranger in the grocery store who insists on arguing with you about how your twins must be identical even though you've clearly said they're not. (And those people do exist, trust me). That's when you have to let them know the conversation is over.

Set Conversational Limits

Sometimes, having a positive attitude will only get you so far. When someone asks you overly personal questions or offers hurtful "advice" or comments, you may need to set conversational limits and send a clear message that his or her comments are unwanted.

Tell Them Straight Out It Bothers You

It may not be the easiest thing to do, but telling someone her comment is bothersome, unwanted, or hurtful is very empowering. It also helps clue in people who are just plain too dumb to pick up on the fact they've crossed a line. A simple statement such as, "I'd appreciate it if you didn't comment on how much weight I've gained, because it hurts my feelings," or "My spouse and I are in the best position to decide how to care for our children," will get your message across.

Change the Subject

When a colleague makes a snide remark such as, "I hope you're not planning to have more kids," or asks if you're going to breast-feed your twins, simply ignore the remark and change the subject. If for some reason the person persists, pause, then say in a slightly louder voice, "As I was saying about the project. . . ." Your colleague will get the message.

Walk Away

It's unfortunate, but sometimes people really do cross the line and say things that are extremely insensitive. And sometimes, given your raging hormones during pregnancy and the stress combined with lack of sleep when your twins are babies, it doesn't take much to set you off or to make you want to cry. This is when you need to remove yourself from the situation and walk away from a troubling conversation. This tactic is pretty much the epitome of setting conversational limits. By walking away, you've effectively communicated that the conversation can go no further.

Give Them a Withering Glare

There are, of course, nonverbal cues that communicate, "Hey, you've gone too far." Case in point is the withering glare, directed at the person who is insensitive enough to pry about how you got pregnant with twins in the first place or whether your boy-girl twins have different fathers (don't laugh, people actually say this stuff). Glare away, but accept that the offender may not actually interpret the glare as you intended it. People may, for example, simply think you don't understand what they've said and repeat themselves, or they may ask if you're tired because you look so funny. (I had people say both of these things to me when I tried the glare move.)

THE FINE ART OF THE WITTY RETORT

So how do pregnant women and parents of twins respond to the weird or rude comments they often receive? I spoke with women to gauge their reactions, and their responses were either sincere answers to the questions or sarcastic replies, usually said with a laugh to soften the edge. (Pregnant women do seem to get away with being extra cranky.) Like a withering glare, a sarcastic remark is most effective when someone picks up on your intent. When people say they feel sorry for you because you have twins, responding with a sarcastic "Thanks, I really appreciate your sympathy" can stop the conversation in its tracks. But once again, sarcasm does not affect the clueless. Here are some real-life examples of questions and comebacks:

* Do twins run in your family? *"Yes, we have twins on both sides." "They do now."*
* Did you use fertility treatments? *"We did it the old-fashioned way." "Yes, we tried for a very long time before we got lucky." "Are you asking me for a referral?"*
* Are you having twins because you're older? *"Hey, thanks for pointing out that I'm old."*
* Oh, so your eggs are dropping at a faster rate. *"Wow, that's a really bizarre comment."*
* You're only five months along! I wasn't as big as you at nine months! *"I'm just lucky to be so healthy."*
* You're huge! *"I'm pregnant. I'm supposed to look huge." "My doctor says I'm right on target with my weight." "Now that's something I hadn't heard yet."*
* Lady, you look like you're going to pop any minute. *(This comment did not warrant a response beyond my jaw hitting the ground.)*
* Just how many are in there? *"I'm not sure, but at least a dozen."*
* My God, I've never seen a belly so big. *"Wait until you see me after the first trimester!" "I wouldn't be so sure about that, tubby."*
* Can I call you doublewide? *"Can I smack you?"*
* How much weight have you gained? *"Too much!" "Enough about me. How much weight have you gained?"*
* I'll bet you have stretch marks! *"Yes, would you like to see them?"*
* You're starting to get that pregnancy waddle. Real response: *"Oh well, I guess I'm just not as graceful as I used to be."* What my colleague wishes she'd said: *"At least I have an excuse."*
* Were you trying for twins? *"No, but they were a pleasant surprise."*
* Will you have to have a C-section? *"Do I need to let you know now, or can it wait until I get to the hospital?"*
* Are you going to breast-feed? *"I'm not sure." "Never in a million years." "I don't want to discuss it with you."*
* Did you have sex twice? *"No, hundreds of times. And you?"*

* This is it, right? *"Yes, I've got to go now." "Yes, we're done having children."*

* You're going to quit your job, aren't you? *"Why would I do that just when I need more money to support my kids?" "Are you going to support me in my life of luxury?"*

* At least it's not triplets. *"Thank God for small blessings, right?"*

* They look alike—are they identical? *"Um, well, one has a penis and the other one doesn't, so no, they're not identical." "They can't be identical. They're different genders."*

* How do you tell them apart? *"We label them." "I can't. I get them mixed up every day." "One's blond, the other has dark hair. It's not that hard." "I was thinking about getting one of them tattooed."*

* Do they act the same? *"Sometimes." "When they're sleeping."*

* Do they eat at the same time? *"Yes, I have them on a schedule." "No, they eat when they're hungry."*

* Do they wake each other up? *"No, but they wake me up."*

* Do you feed them the same things? *"Yes, breast milk."*

* Oh, they look different. *"They're twins, lady, not clones."*

* Are their personalities the same? *"They're only two months old, so if you mean do they eat, poop, sleep, and cry, then yes, their personalities are the same."*

* You sure have your hands full. *"Yes, thanks for noticing."*

* I feel sorry for you. *"I feel sorry that you're so rude."*

* Thank God I'm not in your shoes. *"My kids thank God, too."*

* You poor thing. *"We're fine."*

* How do you manage? *"With a lot of help."*

* There's no way I'd want to be in your shoes. *"Good, because I'm not giving up this job."*

* I hope you have help! *"We have plenty. Thanks for offering, though."*

* Better you than me. *"Did you actually say that?"*

* I bet your husband was thrilled. *"Yes, he took out an ad in the local paper."*

* You're lucky you got it over with at once. *"It's not over yet. It's just beginning."*

* I wish I had twins. *"Yes, we're blessed."*

* I've always wanted twins. *"Twins are a blast. I hope you have some."*

* So-and-so (my second cousin, my husband's niece, my mom's neighbor's daughter) has twins. *"Really, how interesting."*

* Twins run in my family. *"Oh, good for you."*

* Are you planning to have more? *"No, we're done." "Absolutely, I want a set of triplets next."*

* Are you breast-feeding? *"Are you hungry?"*
* Did you plan to have twins? *"As soon as the doctor told me."*
* Now that you've got one of each, you're done, right? *"Our family is the perfect size."*
* You've got double trouble. *"Why, are you with someone?"*
* Did you have to go into labor twice? *"Are you kidding me? I'm still in labor now."*

SPECIAL SITUATIONS

As if their sometimes-rude comments aren't enough, some people insist on touching you or your babies as well.

When Strangers Touch or Grope Your Belly

Don't be surprised when this happens to you. People you don't know will just reach over and, without warning, touch your belly. The best response is to be firm and say something along the lines of "I'd prefer if you didn't do that." Or, more bluntly, "Please stop touching me." On more than one occasion, I simply took the person's hand and removed it from my belly. And, in one case, I took my hand and put it on the other person's belly, just to show them what it felt like. (It felt so strange to both of us that we both pretty much immediately dropped our hands.)

When Strangers Want to Touch Your Babies

This impulse seems to happen less frequently than belly touching, but I was quite surprised to see people trying to touch my newborn twins. With strangers, I was okay if they touched a foot, but less so if they stroked a cheek or touched a hand, because it was just too likely that my babies would put that hand, with those strange germs or viruses, into their mouths. With family and friends, I insisted everyone wash their hands before holding the babies, and if I suspected anyone had a cold, I fended off the would-be holder by saying my doctor recommended that no one, other than my husband and me, handle our (slightly) preemie twins. (They were thirty-six weeks.)

When strangers reach over to touch your babies, this is where you have to be firm. Tell them politely but unequivocally to stop. "Please don't touch the babies" should suffice. If it doesn't, take your babies and leave.

4

Stocking Up on What You *Really* Need

Do twins really need two of everything, or can you get by with only a few essentials? The answer depends on you and your budget. In truth, there's really no reason to get two of everything—until your children get older and learn that "sharing" is a dirty word. Some items, like car seats, you'll absolutely need to buy in pairs, but other supplies are not so clear-cut. Take cribs, for example. It may seem like a no-brainer—two babies, two cribs, right?—but not all babies sleep apart, and even when they do, they don't have to sleep in a full-fledged crib as soon as they get home from the hospital.

There are certain basic supplies you should have on hand when you bring your twins home from the hospital, from car seats and strollers to bedding, clothing, and bathing and feeding supplies. It's not an exhaustive list, but you need to be able to decide what and how many of each to buy. Here are some suggestions (with recommended quantities in parentheses).

Car Seats and Strollers
✓ Car seats (2–4)
✓ Double stroller (1)

Bedding and Clothes
✓ Crib (1), bassinet (1), and Pack 'n Play (1)
✓ Bassinet sheets (6 or more)
✓ Crib sheets (6 or more)
✓ Multipurpose pads (2–4)
✓ Receiving blankets (12–20)

✓ Larger "swaddling" blankets (6)
✓ Baby pajamas (10 or more)
✓ "Home from the hospital" outfits (2)
✓ Socks (6 pairs)
✓ Baby hats (4)
✓ Baskets or large containers (2–4)

Diaper-Changing Gear
✓ Changing tables or stations (2)
✓ Changing pads (2) and pad covers (4)
✓ Size-one diapers (2–3 cases)
✓ Wipes (1–2 cases)
✓ Diaper pails (2)
✓ Large tubes of diaper cream or ointment (several)
✓ Large container of baby powder with cornstarch (1)
✓ Small plastic containers (1–3)
✓ Diaper backpacks (2–3)
✓ Large zippered plastic freezer bags (1–2 packages)

Bathing
✓ Hooded towels (4–6)
✓ Washcloths (4–6)
✓ Mesh baby bathtub seats (2)
✓ Baby bathtubs or bath sponges (2)

Feeding
✓ Bottles (8 total, but 2–3 different types)
✓ Nipples (3 types)
✓ Bottle brushes (2)
✓ Bottle warmer (1)
✓ Large basket or other container (1)
✓ Insulated lunch bags (2–3)
✓ Larger "lunchbox" or insulated container (1)
✓ Freezable ice packs (several)

Miscellaneous Extras
✓ Chalkboard or dry-erase board (1–2)
✓ Boppy pillows (2)
✓ Baby carriers or slings (2)
✓ Night-lights (2–3)
✓ Baby vibrating, bouncy, or papasan chairs (2)

✓ Baby swing (1)
✓ Rectal thermometers (2) and nasal aspirators (2)
✓ Baby grooming kit (1)
✓ Baby play mats (2)
✓ Exersaucers (2)

Questionable Items
✓ Wipe warmers
✓ Newborn baby clothes
✓ Bottle drying rack
✓ Mesh slings for the baby tubs
✓ Diaper stackers

CAR SEATS AND STROLLERS

You can cut back on a lot of things, but car seats and strollers are not among them. Research what options will suit your family best, then buy the best-quality product you can afford.

Car Seats (2–4)

You will certainly need two car seats to take your babies home from the hospital. But will you need seats for any other vehicle? If so, you may want to buy two car seats and two extra bases for a second car, which you can install and keep "on standby." This way, whenever you switch vehicles, you can simply click the car seats into place rather than reinstalling both the base (which is what holds an infant car seat in place) and the car seat itself. On the other hand, you may want to go ahead and buy four seats if you know that another caregiver, like a grandparent, will need to drive with your children on a regular basis. Then you won't have the hassle of transferring car seats.

But what kind of car seats should you buy? Do you want infant-only seats (which snap into strollers), or do you want convertible seats that accommodate babies as small as five pounds and toddlers up to thirty, forty, or even sixty-five pounds?

For twins, I recommend using infant-only seats because they allow you to carry your babies directly in the seats—two hands, two babies. You won't even have to unstrap them. The seats can also serve as impromptu napping places or can be used to seat one baby while you pick up another. If you're worried about how quickly your babies will outgrow the infant-only seats, remember that given their typically lower (sometimes much lower) birth weights, twins are likely to use the seats longer than singleton babies.

The kind of car seat you choose will also affect the kind of stroller you buy (see the next tip), so it pays to do your research. The top brands mentioned by parents include Britax and Graco, which offer car seats at different price points. Just be sure to research the safety features of the various models.

Double Stroller (1)

The ideal double stroller is the holy grail for many parents of twins. There are a lot of considerations to take into account: Do you want your twins to sit side-by-side, or would you prefer a narrower tandem stroller that can more easily fit through standard-size doorways? Which product will be easier to fold, unfold, and push? Do you want a stroller with stadium seating, where the backseat is slightly raised? Or perhaps you'd prefer an all-terrain or jogging stroller? If you have other children, how can you accommodate them if they're too young to walk? Should you invest in a stroller "travel system" that includes a stroller and an infant car seat, or should you go for a frame stroller that accommodates your car seats? Given all of these options, not to mention the high cost of some stroller models (easily $400 to $500 or more), it's no wonder people think long and hard about this issue. Here are some favorites of the parents interviewed for this book.

The Snap-N-Go Infant Car Seat Stroller from Baby Trend is excellent. It's really a lightweight, foldable metal frame that accommodates your infant car seats and provides some storage space for your stuff. Rather than removing your babies from their car seats (which can be a real pain in the winter), like you would have to do with a standard stroller, you simply snap the car seats into place in the frame. Pretty much everyone I know with twins has used this stroller, at least for the first few months. Its advantages are price (it retails for around $100), portability, and user-friendliness. Mothers who had C-sections had no issues lifting it, because it's very lightweight and essentially just "pops up" when you open the frame. On the downside, your babies will outgrow this stroller when they outgrow their car seats, which can be as little as three or as many as six months.

Moms just rave about the Graco DuoGlider, especially because it's very affordable (you can find one in stores for less than $200). It's a tandem-style stroller, which means your babies will ride one behind the other, and it provides stadium seating, so the backseat is slightly raised. Although both seats recline, only the backseat fully reclines. The stroller provides a lot of storage room and is compatible with the Graco SafeSeat or SnugRide (which cost $80–$130 each), so you can take your babies from car to stroller without disturbing them. The DuoGlider is not light. It's also quite long and bulky when folded.

Other brands recommended by parents of twins include the Mountain Buggy Urban Double, the MacLaren Twin Rally (or the newer model, The Twin Triumph), the BOB Revolution (jogging stroller), and the Valco double stroller.

If you have twins plus an older child, I highly recommend the Valco Runabout TriMode Twin, a side-by-side stroller. Parents of twins who have an older child that still likes or needs to ride in a stroller generally had only two options: Buy a stroller that offers a little platform in the back for the oldest child to stand on, or splurge for a triple stroller. I didn't like either of these solutions, so I researched and found this Valco model, which offers a special toddler seat that attaches to the front of the stroller. My two-and-a-half-year-old daughter rode in the attached front seat while the twins reclined in the back, which meant that I could take all three kids for a walk by myself. People would constantly stop us on the street and ask me where we got the stroller. The Valco is extremely easy to assemble (it took me less than ten minutes to put it together), folds and unfolds like a dream, and handles beautifully (all four wheels rotate separately, so you can swivel it really easily). The only downsides are the price (around $650, plus another $100 for the toddler seat) and the weight, around thirty-five pounds. Even though we were on a budget, we splurged on this item, and I have never regretted spending so much on a stroller.

BEDDING AND CLOTHES

Just because you have two babies doesn't mean you have to have two of everything—at least at first. Let's go through your must-haves for sleeping gear and clothing.

Crib (1), Bassinet (1), and Pack 'n Play (1)

Notice that I didn't say two cribs, two bassinets, or two Pack 'n Plays. The truth is that your babies will not need a crib right away. They just need two separate places to sleep, especially if you and your spouse are sharing the nighttime feedings or taking shifts with each baby.

Many parents of twins have both babies sleep together in the same crib, not just for space reasons, but because they believe the babies will be comforted having their twin right next to them, as if they were still in the womb. If that's something you are considering, you should definitely be able to manage with a single crib for the first three months or so.

You also don't necessarily need two bassinets, because you can mix and match sleeping places (crib, bassinet, and Pack 'n Play) for the first two or three months. The real issue is to make sure you have at least two places for the babies to sleep so that you can separate them if necessary. Preparing multiple places for the babies to sleep was among the best tips I ever received when I was pregnant with my twins. We frequently brought one or both of our twins downstairs to sleep so that our toddler daughter would not be disturbed by the babies' crying.

Pack 'n Plays are more portable than bassinets. They are basically light-weight playpens that can serve multiple functions: They are suitable as a sleeping area, play area, changing table (many brands come with a separate changing-table attachment), and portable crib on vacations or sleepovers at grandma's house. Definitely invest in at least one Pack 'n Play, either to use in place of a crib or bassinet for one of the babies, or to use as a "holding area" in case you need to put one of the babies down quickly. A colleague of mine, a parent of twins, kept a Pack 'n Play inside her house, right by her door, so she had a safe and convenient place to bring in one baby while she went back to her car to get the other. Another friend with twins keeps one by her extra changing area, so she always has a place to set down one of her boys while taking care of the other.

Bassinet Sheets (6 or More)

If you're planning to use a bassinet (or two, for that matter), make sure you have at least six bassinet sheets: You'll need one set for immediate use, one set in case you're doing laundry, and one set as a spare, because inevitably, as soon as you're doing laundry, your babies will spit up, pee, or spill something. If you limit yourself to four sheets, you'll really wish you had the extra set so that you can change the babies' sheets when necessary, without waiting for the set in the laundry to be washed and dried.

Crib Sheets (6 or More)

For the same reasons, you'll want to have at least six crib sheets, and possibly even more. Once we bought them, we used them for years. I never bought another crib sheet beyond what I bought when I was pregnant or what I got at my baby shower. But make sure you buy good-quality sheets. Spend extra initially and you'll save money in the long run by not having to replace inexpensive sheets that will fall apart from the frequent washings.

Multipurpose Pads (2–4)

Similar to burp cloths, these pads are meant to protect you and your clothes from baby spit-up. They're generally sold in the feeding accessories section of baby stores, but you should also consider them essential bedding items. They are excellent over-the-sheet liners for your crib or bassinet mattress. Basically, you place one of these pads on top of your crib or bassinet mattress, right over the sheet, and place your baby on top. Then, if one or both of your twins spits up, you won't have to strip the bed and wash the sheet. Instead, just remove the small pad and wash that. You can also use cloth diapers or receiving blankets for the same purpose.

Receiving Blankets (12–20)

Why so many? Because receiving blankets are not only great for swaddling babies, but you'll find plenty of other uses for them. They make excellent over-the-shoulder burp cloths, for instance. Folded or rolled into a tube, they can help support your babies' heads in their car seats. Rolled up, they are also fantastic bottle props (yes, I know, I know, bottle propping is not ideal, but you'll find it is necessary with twins). Frankly, the best baby blankets are those we used in the hospital—they are soft, absorbent, thick but not too bulky, and just the perfect size—but since you have to buy your own, stick with blankets made of soft cotton flannel rather than either fleece (warm, but tougher to swaddle babies in) or crocheted (tough for swaddling, and not as absorbent).

Larger "Swaddling" Blankets (6)

You'll discover that your babies love to be swaddled. Many infants desire swaddling much longer than the week or two you might typically assume. In addition, because twins are often born prematurely, they need the extra warmth and comfort provided by swaddling for a longer period of time. At some point, your babies will outgrow the standard-size receiving blanket (which measures roughly thirty to thirty-six inches). If you're still swaddling your babies when they are three, five, or even nine months old, make your own larger swaddling blankets out of flannel cloth (or have someone make them for you).

Baby Pajamas (10 or More)

Your babies will spend most of their time in pajamas, not clothes, so you'll need plenty for extra changes. It's not unusual for one baby to go through three pajamas a day. Times two, that's six pajamas per day, plus you may have to count one extra change during the night. With ten pajamas, you'll still be doing laundry nearly every day, but at least you'll have enough items on hand initially, until you are able to buy more after you get home from the hospital.

Of that ten, make sure at least two or three are baby gowns and another two or three are zippered pajamas. Then you'll be able to experiment the first few nights to see which type of pajama—the gown or the zippered outfit—you and your babies prefer for night changes. Avoid pajamas with snaps for the nighttime.

Let me share my experience (in time, you'll have your own funny story to tell): One of the reasons we preferred to use zippered pajamas instead of baby gowns was that one of our twins was a squirmer. Within minutes, he could wiggle free not just from the swaddling, but from his clothes. One day, when he was about ten days old, we discovered him scrunched up against the top of his bassinet, naked except for his diaper, while his swaddling blanket was at his feet. It was as if someone had peeled a banana by pushing it upward!

"Home from the Hospital" Outfits (2)

Your babies may spend most of their time in pajamas, but you will definitely want cute outfits for their trip home from the hospital. These are probably the only clothes you may want to purchase in a preemie size (just keep the store tags, in case your babies end up too big to fit into preemie sizes). Another option is to find outfits you like, then write down the product/brand names, store name, and SKU information so that your spouse, mom, sister, or friend can purchase them in the appropriate size while you're in the hospital.

Socks (6 Pairs)

Lets face it, there's not much reason to change a baby's socks. It's not like they're walking anywhere, so the socks aren't getting dirty. Baby socks are typically used to keep the babies' feet warm, so you'll definitely want to have some on hand, but early on you don't really need many pairs. Most parents just reuse the socks for multiple wearings.

Baby Hats (4)

Yes, they are must-haves, but two baby hats per child should suffice, mostly to cover those situations when you've misplaced the hat your baby was just wearing a second ago. Hats also come in handy if you have identical twins and want to distinguish who is who easily.

Baskets or Large Containers (2–4)

There will be lots of stuff to corral: baby hats and socks, receiving blankets and pacifiers. Sure, you'll probably have a dresser with lots of drawers in their bedroom, but you'll really need a few containers for areas of the house where your babies live, not just sleep, such as your living or family room.

Think also about getting containers that will look good with your home's overall décor, not just the décor of your babies' room.

DIAPER-CHANGING GEAR

Because diaper changing is going to consume much of your time, be prepared and stock up ahead of time. The following are indispensable items from day one.

Changing Tables or Stations (2)

Make sure you have two changing stations. Don't worry about buying a specific type of changing table, because there's no one "right" kind. Changing tables can be specially designed dressers with a built-in changing area, a Pack 'n Play with an adjustable changing area, or a standard stand-alone changing table. The purpose of having two changing stations is not so much because there may be times when both babies need to be changed simultaneously (although this will happen often), but because you'll want two changing tables in different areas of your house for your own convenience. If, for example, one baby is sleeping and you need to change the other, you don't have to walk into the twins' bedroom or sleeping area to do it. Also, if you live in a large or multilevel house, or if you know you'll be having a C-section and won't want to do a lot of unnecessary walking after the babies are born, it makes sense to have multiple changing areas positioned where they are most convenient for you. Finally, if you set up a secondary changing area in your main living area (whether family room or living room), you'll have a better chance of getting your spouse to pitch in with diaper changes.

Changing Pads (2) and Pad Covers (4)

If you have two changing tables, you will need changing pads and covers. Get one extra cover for each pad so that you can launder one when it gets dirty.

Size-One Diapers (2–3 Cases)

Skip the preemie diapers. You'll get plenty of tiny diapers at the hospital (the nursing staff generally sends you home with two diaper bags, bottles of formula, and as many diapers as you can carry), and when you go through those, then you can stock up. Buy at least two or even three cases of the size-one diapers. You'll easily go through ten to fifteen diapers a day. A single case will last you ten days, maximum.

Wipes (1–2 Cases)

You will go through *a lot* of wipes. The last thing you're going to want to do is constantly run to the store to replenish them. For my family, as well as a number of other mothers I interviewed, the cost of a Costco membership (about $50 a year) was worth it just for the wipes alone: The Kirkland Signature brand wipes (Costco's house brand) are hands-down the best wipes we ever used, and they're sold by the case. Most other brands found in the grocery or drugstore are sold in packages of two, which is barely enough to get you home before you run out!

Diaper Pails (2)

Since the diaper pail will almost immediately become the most used item in your house, try to buy a brand that does a good job of keeping out odors and lets you use regular garbage bags rather than pricey refills. Many moms of twins recommend Baby Trend's Diaper Champ. Buy at least two diaper pails so that you can have them in two different locations (upstairs and downstairs) and reduce the number of times you're changing the bags by half.

Large Tubes of Diaper Cream or Ointment (Several)

Favorite brands of diaper creams/ointments, according to the moms I spoke with, are Boudreaux's Butt Paste, Desitin Creamy ointment (our personal favorite), Weleda diaper care cream (available at Whole Foods), and Triple Paste.

Ointments tend to be more effective than creams because an ointment provides a thicker barrier for your babies' bottoms. But the cream or ointment you choose also has to be spreadable.

Large Container of Baby Powder with Cornstarch (1)

You may find yourself in a situation where you don't like *any* diaper creams, so have some cornstarch baby powder on hand as an alternative.

Small Plastic Containers (1–3)

Small plastic containers are great to house all of the stuff—the creams, ointments, alcohol wipes, Q-Tips, and baby nail clippers—that you're sure to accumulate near your changing area. Avoid the baby "junk drawer" phenomenon and manage the mess by storing everything in a container that's small enough to sit on your dresser or on the top shelf of your changing table.

Diaper Backpacks (2–3)

Many mothers of twins swear by backpacks because they provide more room and organizational compartments than a standard diaper bag. I'd have to agree. I had several diaper bags and none worked as well as a backpack. The bags were generally too small and I could never find anything I actually needed. I'd always end up digging in and then dumping out the bag in my car, or even on the floor of a public restroom, as I struggled to find that elusive diaper or wipe. Remember, you'll be carrying almost twice as much stuff as moms or dads of singleton babies, so storage space is a premium! In addition, because backpacks are designed to be worn on your back, they leave your arms free to push a stroller or hold two babies.

If you do end up getting diaper bags, make sure you test-drive them in the store first: Put several bottles, toys, blankets, and a container of wipes, as well as your keys, wallet, and phone into the bag and walk around with it. Do the straps stay in place while you're bending over to pick something off a shelf or off the ground? Is the bag heavy or cumbersome? Dig around in the bag. Can you find your keys? Does the bag expand easily if you want to add more stuff?

Large Zippered Plastic Freezer Bags (1–2 Packages)

Large zippered plastic freezer bags are great because you can use them to store extra wipes (so you don't have to carry a whole package of wipes); to create "quick change" bags of diapers, wipes, and lotion; to prevent leakage from bottles of milk; and to hold dirty diapers (if you can't immediately throw them away).

BATHING

Giving your twins a bath is challenging enough without having to worry that you're missing some essential item while you're holding a wet and slippery baby. Stick with the basics and you'll be fine.

Hooded Towels (4–6)

Hooded towels are not just some gimmicky item sold to new parents. They're indispensable for keeping your babies' heads warm after their baths. Unfortunately, many of the towels commonly sold are so thin they might as well be oversize washcloths. If possible, buy thicker hooded towels—the thicker, the better—even if they're somewhat large. Both Pottery Barn Kids and Lillian Vernon sell these items, as do a slew of specialty baby and boutique stores. If you are into crafts or do-it-yourself projects(or know someone who is), you can also make your own by cutting off a section of the towel and reattaching it as a hood. It's worth investing some money in these towels, because you will use them nearly every day for several years.

Washcloths (4–6)

Do not become overloaded with washcloths until you discover that you happen to use them. Washcloths are one of those items that people like giving with their baby shower gifts—they're the baby shower version of stocking stuffers. But if you don't happen to like using washcloths, they will just sit there taking up space in your dresser. Wait until you give your babies a couple of baths before getting more.

Mesh Baby Bathtub Seats (2)

These little seats are truly practical, because you can either give your babies a sponge bath while they are in the seat, or you can temporarily "park" a baby in one of the seats on the bathroom floor while you wash the other baby. The seats are made of mesh, so they dry easily after getting wet. But be aware that if you do use them as bathroom baby seats, the seats recline a bit and very young babies can slowly slide off them if you're not paying close attention. Because of this sliding danger, don't put the seats on any elevated surface. I learned this lesson the hard way when one of my twins slid progressively further toward the floor during the few minutes I took to wash her brother. Luckily, she was already on the floor and had nowhere to go, and I picked her up before she could slide down too much. So why did I continue to use the seats? I really liked them. They were compact enough so that I could have two seats in my small bathroom and I always had a comfortable place for one of the babies to sit.

Baby Bathtubs or Bath Sponges (2)

The biggest benefit of having two baby bathtubs is that you and your spouse can separately and simultaneously wash each of the twins. It's worth it, trust me. If you don't have the space for baby bathtubs, get two large baby bath sponges instead (you'll find them in the bathing section at Babies "R" Us).

FEEDING

Chapters 8 and 9, respectively, cover breast- and bottle-feeding in detail, including the essential items you'll need. In the meantime, if you plan on bottle-feeding, here's a brief rundown of items you should have on hand before bringing your twins home. (I also recommend having some of these items on hand even if you plan to breast-feed, just in case you run into any kind of problems.)

Bottles (8 Total, but 2–3 Different Types)

There is some controversy about the safety of plastic baby bottles, which have been found to leach a harmful chemical called bisphenol A into liquids and food. In 2007, the FDA affirmed the safety of plastic baby bottles, but be sure to do your research before deciding which types of bottles you're comfortable using. Your twins are individuals and may like different styles of bottles. Buy only a few, but buy different types so that you can mix and match the bottle to the baby if necessary.

Nipples (3 Types)

Like bottles, nipples come in multiple designs. But you'll only need to buy a few; just buy them in different styles.

Bottle Brushes (2)

If you're using bottles, you'll need to clean them. Get a couple of brushes to keep by the sink (they can get gunky fast).

Bottle Warmer (1)

A bottle warmer can be terrific (especially at night), but you definitely won't need two of them, because warming bottles in hot water is generally faster. That said, a bottle warmer is great to have as backup; in the winter, it may take a while for your water to heat up, or at other times you may need to warm bottles away from a sink.

Large Basket or Other Container (1)

With twins, your house will quickly be overrun with baby paraphernalia such as bottles, nipples, and pacifiers. These items don't store well in a cabinet—they're small, oddly shaped, and prone to falling over. Find a basket or other type of container and keep it on a counter. Alternatively, you can purchase a bottle rack for storing your bottles, but then you'll still have to deal with bottle liners, nipples, and bottle caps.

Insulated Lunch Bags (2–3)

If you leave the house with your twins and you need to feed them, insulated lunch bags are the way to go. They're compact and you can close them, which means you won't have to worry about spills. Plus, if you pop in some ice packs, they do a great job of keeping formula and breast milk fresh and cold. Have two or three small bags on hand to use in a pinch. Put a small bag in your backpack, in your purse, or in your stroller. Buy a larger size for longer trips (they're also great for carrying your drinks and food, not just your babies' formula).

Larger "Lunchbox" or Insulated Container (1)

Get one larger insulated container, suitable for packing a small picnic lunch or multiple bottles. It comes in very handy on longer errands and day trips.

We were able to pack at least eight bottles in ours, plus ice packs, yogurt or baby food, spoons, and wipes and napkins. A larger picnic-type container also worked well when our babies were older and we took them to the park or the zoo in a wagon rather than a stroller.

Freezable Ice Packs (Several)
Buy five or six freezable ice packs in different sizes and keep them handy in your freezer.

MISCELLANEOUS EXTRAS

There are a lot of things you don't necessarily think about until you need them. They include the following items.

Chalkboard or Dry-Erase Board (1–2)
Chalkboards and dry erase boards are fantastic items for parents of twins because they let you easily track feedings and diaper changes. A centralized tracking system is especially important if you and your spouse are splitting the work.

Boppy Pillows (2)
Boppy pillows offer the perfect support for your babies when you are trying to feed them both simultaneously (they are not, however, intended for sleeping). During feedings, we would place the pillows on the floor, then place a baby in each of them.

Baby Carriers or Slings (2)
Since you will likely have to be alone with your babies on occasion, carriers or slings are must-haves, because they leave your hands free.

Night-Lights (2–3)
Put night-lights in your bedroom, the hallway, and the kitchen or bathroom. There's nothing worse than stumbling around in the dark trying to prepare bottles or change diapers, and you certainly want to avoid turning on bright lights during nighttime feedings. Although babies sleep better in darker rooms, night-lights are imperative, even if you only put them in a hallway right outside of their room.

Baby Vibrating, Bouncy, or Papasan Chairs (2)
Vibrating or bouncy chairs are indispensable, even if you don't use the vibrating option. (Papasan chairs are like bouncy or vibrating chairs, without

the vibrating option.) With twins you will be always be looking for places to set down one baby while you pick up the other. These chairs are great. Buy at least two, and maybe even three, just to have them in multiple places around the house.

Baby Swing (1)
Many people decide to buy two swings right off the bat, but since there's no guarantee your babies will like them, you may be left with a white elephant item that takes up a lot of room. Buy (or borrow) one swing to start, then get a second if your twins love it.

Rectal Thermometers (2) and Nasal Aspirators (2)
Rectal thermometers and nasal aspirators are generally included in baby "healthcare" kits, which usually also contain nail clippers and an oral medicine syringe. You don't actually need two kits, just two of the items that you don't want your babies to share for health reasons, like a rectal thermometer and an aspirator. Be aware, however, that the hospital will send you home with the aspirators your twins used when they were born, so you probably won't need to purchase additional aspirators unless you want extras around.

Baby Grooming Kit (1)
Baby grooming kits are cute: You get a little hairbrush and comb, some nail clippers, and nail scissors. But you don't need two kits.

Baby Play Mats (2)
Although they are not among the first things you will want to have on hand after your babies are born, baby play mats are excellent toys and it pays to have two of them, that way you can keep them in different areas of your house, plus you'll be able to give each baby enough play space. Play mats (one popular brand is the Tiny Love Gymini) have attached toys for your babies to look at and later to reach for, and they offer a great option for when you need to put your babies down, since you just lay them down on the floor. I would often lay one or both of my twins down on a play mat while I ate dinner or folded laundry.

Exersaucers (2)
These are great items to get as a gift at your shower, even if your babies won't use them for a few months (unlike play mat toys that can be used from birth). Exersaucers are stationary play areas where your babies sit upright in a seat surrounded by a number of toys they can push, grab, or rattle—they're little baby entertainment centers! The toys are intended for babies around

four or five months of age, who can sit upright and have good head control. The cost can be fairly high, around $99, but an Exersaucer is completely and utterly worth it, because your babies can play with it for an extended period of time for months on end.

QUESTIONABLE ITEMS

Parents-to-be often get swept up in the mentality that their babies need everything that manufacturers of baby products say they do. Unfortunately, you'll have to discover on your own which of the many available baby products you really need, because one person's must-have is another person's don't-bother. However, there are some items you really won't need.

Wipe Warmers
In my opinion, wipe warmers are a total waste of money. If you're thinking wipe warmers will make diaper changes more comfortable for your babies, remember that the whole diaper-changing experience is pretty disruptive for them. Modifying one step out of several is not going to make much of a difference. Most of the mothers I spoke with panned this item.

Newborn Baby Clothes
Other than their going-home outfits, your babies will live in their pajamas for the first two or three months. Save yourself some money and wait to purchase clothes until your babies are older.

Bottle Drying Rack
Wait a while before you buy a bottle drying rack. You may breast-feed exclusively, and even if you do bottle-feed, you may discover that your dishwasher rack works just fine.

Mesh Slings for the Baby Tubs
Mesh slings are usually sold along with the baby tub and are meant to attach to the tub edge and provide support for your baby. However, they are hard to use and they get a horrible mildewy smell very quickly. Skip them.

Diaper Stackers
Diaper stackers are intended to store and display your diapers neatly. The box or bag the diapers come in works much better.

5

Preparing and Involving Your Other Children

If you think having twins will disrupt your world, just think how disruptive it will be for your other child (or children). Up until now, your son or daughter has been the center of your life, the apple of your eye, and now, in one fell swoop, he or she is going to be forced to share the spotlight. What's more, this spotlight will relentlessly shine on the new babies for a long time to come. They're sweet, they're cute, and there are two of them. On a more serious note, if your new babies happen to have serious health issues, you will probably be unable to give your other children the same level of attention that they are accustomed to simply because of the demands on your time and the stress on your emotions. It's no wonder that having two new siblings can be a traumatic experience for a previous child.

On the other hand, with some effort and preparation on your part, the birth of your twins can be the beginning of a wonderful relationship for all of you. You can manage the transition by preparing your child (or children, of course) for the impending changes, involving him in the new routines, making her continue to feel special even as the babies receive their share of attention, and being flexible in your expectations of what your child should and should not be doing. Here are some suggestions:

Preparing Your Child
✓ Introduce change early.
✓ Make incremental changes.
✓ Keep the explanations coming.
✓ Use dolls or toys to introduce the concept of twins.
✓ Read your child stories about twins.

✓ Visit someone with babies.

✓ Don't spring the babies on your child.

Involving Your Older Child

✓ Create a book of family stories to share with the babies.

✓ Draw artwork for the babies' room.

✓ Contribute something special to a quilt.

✓ Include older children in your new routines.

✓ Make a game of naming the babies.

Making Your Child Feel Special

✓ Greet your child first when you come home from the hospital.

✓ Bring home a gift "from the babies."

✓ Assemble a photo album.

✓ Create a personalized storybook.

✓ Frame and display a picture.

✓ Play up the "big brother" or "big sister" theme.

✓ Develop a new "special" bedtime routine.

✓ Acknowledge and celebrate your older child's milestones.

✓ Make a date with your older child.

✓ Set aside daily "alone" time with your older child.

✓ Declare some things "off-limits" to the twins.

✓ Celebrate differences.

✓ Keep a secret stash of gifts.

✓ Arrange play dates.

Adjusting Your Expectations

✓ Don't force the "big sister" or "big brother" role.

✓ Watch for copycat behavior (it's normal).

✓ Expect ongoing jealousy (it's normal, too).

PREPARING YOUR CHILD

Your child (or children) will be better equipped to weather the changes in your family if they have opportunities to understand and become familiar with them.

Introduce Change Early

Everyday routines tend to flow fairly uninterrupted in a family that's expecting twins—until the babies come home. Then chaos hits and the routines go out the window. Unfortunately, as you might imagine, this situation is very troubling for most children, who depend on routines for stability. You can minimize disruptions by introducing change *before* the babies come home. For example, if you know your other child will have to move to a different bedroom, don't wait until you come home from the hospital with two screaming, demanding infants to initiate the bedroom switch. Not only is that harder on you, since you'll have your hands full enough as it is, but having your child move earlier will be much easier on him or her, because your son or daughter won't associate the babies' arrival with the confusing (and generally unwanted) changes in his or her life.

Make Incremental Changes

As a corollary to the previous tip, keep transitions smooth by making changes in increments. If your daughter will have to move to a different room, start preschool, or get used to a different caretaker shortly after your twins are born, begin acclimating her to those different circumstances in small bits. Let her choose the paint color in her new room. Carry only one or two pieces of furniture in first (a chair, perhaps, or a table where she can draw), or let her take naps on the floor in a sleeping bag before you go all out and move her to her new room. Similarly, if she has to start preschool because you need to take care of the twins (as happened with our daughter), start early and have her go part-time for a few weeks before the babies are born. The point is to avoid abrupt and rapid change before (and after) your twins are born. Once your babies are home, don't abruptly stop routines you've been doing previously; taper them off instead.

Keep the Explanations Coming

Because young children have short attention spans, your discussions and explanations of how your family will grow should be an ongoing dialogue that intensifies as your due date draws near. Your other children benefit from this approach, although at some point you'll probably want to limit the twin talk so that you can enjoy the time with your family as it currently exists.

Use Dolls or Toys to Introduce the Concept of Twins

For her second birthday, three months before our twins were born, we gave our daughter a twin stroller with boy-and-girl twin dolls to get her used to the idea of having both a brother and a sister. We emphasized how mommy had two babies in her tummy and would soon have two babies and a stroller just like her. If your son is not interested in dolls, he may be interested in teddy bear twins.

Read Your Child Stories About Twins

Although there are a ton of books about twins, very few are directed at siblings of twins. Instead, the books generally show what it's like to be a twin.

That said, *Twinnies* by Eve Bunting (1997) is a great book for an older sibling. It tells the story of a six-year-old girl and how hard it is to be the big sister of twins. You may be able to find a copy online or at your local library. Younger children will enjoy books that simply feature twins as characters. Three great choices are *Hello Twins* by Charlotte Voake (which tells the story of boy-girl twins), *Twins!* by Charlotte Doyle (2003), and *Twin to Twin* by Margaret O'Hair and Thierry Courtin (2003).

Visit Someone with Babies

Let your son or daughter learn about twin babies the "up-close and personal" way—by visiting someone with a baby and showing your child what babies are all about. Ideally, to get the full effect of the experience, you should visit another family with twins (this is where getting involved in a twins club or support group could really help you out).

Don't Spring the Babies on Your Child

A lot of parents will arrange a sleepover for their child (or children) while they go to the hospital for the delivery. If you do a special sleepover for your other children, make sure they are home when you bring home the babies, so they don't come back to a radically altered environment. It's better to let them see and welcome the babies rather than walk into a house where everything seems to have changed.

INVOLVING YOUR OLDER CHILD

Your children will feel better about becoming the older siblings if they feel included and invested in the experience. Involve your other child or children as you prepare your home for the twins' arrival.

Create a Book of Family Stories to Share with the Babies

For younger children, creating a book of family stories can be as simple as having them draw some pictures of you, your spouse, grandparents, aunts or uncles, pets, house, or anything else that represents your family. You can then collect their drawings in a presentation folder or binder or "stitch" them together by hole-punching the pages and weaving a ribbon through the holes. If your children are old enough to tell or write a story, you can go a step further and write captions on the pages. Have them dedicate the book to the babies.

Older children can do a more sophisticated version by writing a story on the computer and illustrating it with family photographs or scanned pictures of their drawings. If you want to go all out, there are commercial options as well, including a great product called IlluStory. It's an activity kit that lets children draw pictures and write a short story on special pages that are then sent off to the publisher and bound, so the end-product looks like a real book. Various websites such as www.Shutterfly.com also let you create photo books with captions.

Draw Artwork for the Babies' Room
From handprints to crayon masterpieces to wall murals, your children can create art for the babies' room. This is not only be a great decorating option, but it will make your other children feel truly special to have contributed to something that everyone can see and enjoy in the twins' room. Just be sure to frame it and present it nicely.

Contribute Something Special to a Quilt
If you are a quilter or know someone who is making quilts for your babies, let your babies' sibling choose an item of clothing or a piece of a special blanket that will be incorporated into the quilt. Explain what a special gift this is to the babies and how much they will love and appreciate having something from their brother or sister.

Include Older Children in Your New Routines
Instead of letting your other son or daughter feel left out while you're busy with the babies, draw him or her into the new routines you are developing. Let your child hold the babies if possible. If you're nursing the twins, have your child bring you burp cloths. If you're reading to the babies, have your child sit on your lap or on the arm of the chair. In our household, it was our toddler's job to hand me towels while I gave the twins a bath. It wasn't that hard to do and it made her feel like she was as important to me as she'd ever been. Other suggestions include having your child pick out books you can read to the babies or choose the toys that belong in the twins' room.

Make a Game of Naming the Babies
Brainstorm with your child about baby names, and have your son or daughter suggest names for his or her new siblings. I'm not advocating that you put your children in charge of naming your twins, but ask for their opinions, have them "vote" on the best names, or discuss what the names mean.

MAKING YOUR CHILD FEEL SPECIAL

Everybody loves to comment on twins, but your other children want acknowledgment as well. Make an extra effort to pay special attention to them, so they don't end up feeling eclipsed by the twins. Bribery works, too!

Greet Your Child First When You Come Home from the Hospital

Hand off your babies to your spouse, or leave the babies in their car seats so you can greet your child or children without the babies in your arms. This "hands-free" greeting will go a long way to making your children feel they have your undivided attention.

Bring Home a Gift "from the Babies"

We stole the idea of bringing home a gift "from the babies" from some friends of ours. In our case, we bought an inflatable castle (a kind of bouncy activity toy) for our basement, wrapped the box, and kept it in the car until we came home with the babies. Then we walked in the door not just with our twins, but with a big box for our oldest daughter and announced the babies brought her a present. Sure enough, she focused more on the gift than on the babies, and the new toy gave us an opportunity to remind her how much the babies loved her because they had gotten her such an awesome gift.

Assemble a Photo Album

An album of individual photos of my oldest daughter is one of her most cherished items. She looks at it often and asks questions about when she was a baby. It also showcases lots of moments before the babies were born and reminds her (and us) of when our family just included the three of us and she was our newest addition.

Create a Personalized Storybook

There are plenty of resources online that allow you to create and purchase personalized storybooks. The books incorporate your child's name and personal details into the narrative, and some books will also use your child's image. We love a book we purchased from a company called Make It About Me! (which has since been acquired by Shutterfly). You create the book online by choosing one of several prepared stories, then scanning in a photo of your child. The book that arrives a couple of weeks later will truly delight you and your child.

Frame and Display a Picture

When the babies come home, you'll take tons of pictures and, most likely, so will your family. In addition, you'll probably be sending birth announcements of the twins. Amid all this, your older child will be feeling less special than before. Increase the attention level by taking an updated photo of your child. Then buy a nice frame and display it in a prominent place in your home where all your visitors can see it.

Play Up the "Big Brother" or "Big Sister" Theme

If your child is enthused about being known as the big brother or big sister, indulge him or her with "big brother" and "big sister" themed goods, such as T-shirts and hats. Beyond clothes, you can post a sign on your child's bedroom door that tells everyone this is "big sibling territory." But take your cues from your child—play up the "big sister" or "big brother" theme as long as your child is comfortable. If you go overboard, your child may end up feeling pushed aside as the baby of the family.

Develop a New "Special" Bedtime Routine

If your children's current bedtime routine is disrupted by the arrival of your twins, develop a new routine that either includes them in the twins-oriented action or that emphasizes their uniqueness. As my twins grew into toddlers and my oldest entered preschool, I had all three of my children bathe together, and then I read to all of them, first in the babies' room, followed by a special story just for my oldest right before she went to bed. Another mom I talked to began letting her five-year-old help prepare dinner as a way to compensate for their reduced nighttime routine.

Acknowledge and Celebrate Your Older Child's Milestones

Just as you celebrate the babies' milestones—turning over, smiling, getting a first tooth—celebrate the accomplishments of your older child, too. For example, if your son passes a spelling test or masters a chore, praise him and share the news. Some moms give stickers; others make a point of calling grandma. One mom created and displayed on her refrigerator door a certificate of accomplishment when her daughter learned to spell her first and last name. These are very small celebrations, but important to your child, nonetheless.

Make a Date with Your Older Child

Nothing beats the undivided attention of mom and dad, but with two new babies in the house, that's next to impossible. Schedule a recurring activity with your older children to make sure they have some time alone with you. It can be as simple as taking your son or daughter to a library story group, taking them grocery shopping with you, or making a weekly movie date.

Set Aside Daily "Alone" Time with Your Older Child

Even if it's only fifteen or thirty minutes, give your singleton child some attention that is not associated with accomplishing a specific goal—like eating dinner or getting ready for a bath. This time together should also be independent of the twins. For example, if you find that the only time you spend alone with your daughter is when she's helping you do something baby-related, it's time to step back and see where you can carve out fifteen minutes or more to focus on her.

Declare Some Things "Off-Limits" to the Twins

Over the years, there will be plenty of occasions when your other child will have to share his toys, his room, or his friends with his younger siblings. Help your children retain a sense of personal space by designating some items as theirs exclusively. The off-limits items can be a blanket, specific toys, or even a place on the sofa at a certain time of day.

Celebrate Differences

It's tough when your younger siblings are constantly in the spotlight, as twins tend to be. But your older child doesn't have to feel excluded. Even very young children can understand there are differences and advantages to being older and a non-twin. Begin a discussion with your other children by asking questions. For example: What are babies good at? What are big kids good at? Why is it nice to be the oldest? What is hard about being twins? Then remind them of the privileges of being older (you get to do more things, stay up later, and know more about the world) and the great things about being a singleton (there's less sharing, for instance, if there's an age difference, and no one will mix him up with his brother).

Keep a Secret Stash of Gifts

Purchase and wrap a selection of inexpensive toys from the dollar store so that if visitors show up and have gifts for the babies, you have a ready supply of items for your other child as well.

Arrange Play Dates

As your twins get older, your other child might begin to feel left out, especially if there's an age difference of four years or more. Arrange play dates so that your child has a companion around her age, rather than expecting her to always play by herself or to entertain her younger siblings.

ADJUSTING YOUR EXPECTATIONS

Just because your son or daughter is older doesn't mean he or she will readily take on a caretaker role or always act mature. It helps if your expectations of your child's behavior aren't unrealistically high.

Don't Force the "Big Sister" or "Big Brother" Role

While children love to feel older and are often protective of their younger siblings, that doesn't mean they always want to act older or protective. Many times they don't want to be the big brother or sister, the one who has to give up their toys, sit patiently while mom and dad take care of the babies, be more understanding, or not hit back when one of the babies pulls their hair. If your children want to regress a bit, especially right after the babies are born, let them.

Watch for Copycat Behavior (It's Normal)

If you have children close in age, be aware that they might want to dress or pretend like they are part of a "set" with the twins—in other words, your twins may become, in a sense, triplets.

Expect Ongoing Jealousy (It's Normal, Too)

Even if your child adjusts really well, there will be plenty of times when he will be jealous of his twin siblings. Twins, especially babies, command and demand a lot of attention. At some point, your child will have had enough of being the third wheel. Expect it and try not to punish him for these normal feelings.

6

Preparing and Involving the Father of the Babies

It's pretty common today to find men who are hands-on parents, who pride themselves on their ability change diapers and give bottles. But truth be told, the majority of the nitty-gritty work of parenting—from night feedings and dressing the baby to setting pediatrician appointments and play dates—still mostly falls to the mom. Unless you have twins, that is.

Two babies demand two full-time adults, at least for the first several months. With a first child, dads may stop getting up in the middle of the night to help with feedings by week two. But with twins, dads will find themselves in for a radical change. Having twins absolutely means both the mom and the dad must be hands-on parents from the moment the babies come home, and in some cases (for example, when the mom is on bed rest), even before.

If you're the dad, how do you prepare for twins? And if you're the mom, how do you get your spouse to be a full-fledged partner in parenting? It's simple: You have to start the process from the moment you learn you're having twins. You can't expect ideal results if the dad only comes on board when you have two screaming infants. Ideal results—in this case, a dad who not only feels capable of doing everything the babies need, but actually does it—come from practice, practice, practice. Here are some tips.

Breaking the News That You're Pregnant
✓ Play down the shock.
✓ Understand his perspective.

What He's Most Worried About
✓ Your health
✓ Your finances

✓ His social life
✓ His sex life
✓ Your expectations
✓ Arranging time off from work
✓ Formulating a plan

During Pregnancy
✓ Take a class.
✓ Become CPR-skilled.
✓ Arrange finances, insurance, and wills.
✓ Divide the research.
✓ Prepare the room.
✓ Arrange the work schedule.
✓ Take advantage of time off.
✓ Max out "guy time."

Hands-On Training
✓ Pack the diaper bag.
✓ Put away supplies.
✓ Buy and prepare formula.
✓ Fold and unfold the stroller.
✓ Install and uninstall the car seats.
✓ Strap in the babies.

After the Babies Are Born
✓ Devise a schedule.
✓ Take nighttime shifts.
✓ Leave him alone with the babies.
✓ Give him time off.

BREAKING THE NEWS THAT YOU'RE PREGNANT

Even if you've prepared for the possibility of multiples since before you got pregnant, twins are always a surprise. The moment you hear the big news is both memorable and fraught with concern. Start things off right by understanding the father's unique perspective and working with it, not against it.

Play Down the Shock
The moment of learning you're having twins seems to defy all preparation. Maybe it's the reality of it all, but no matter how prepared you think you are,

twins inevitably come as a complete and utter shock. After shock comes joy, then panic and fright, then some more joy. Although this yo-yo effect eventually evens out, it does take some time to get used to the idea that you are having multiple babies. In many cases, the mom learns she's having twins first, and then, even as she is digesting the news, she has to tell the father-to-be. This puts him in a tough position. On the one hand, he'll be experiencing the aforementioned yo-yo effect when he hears for the first time that you're having twins. On the other, he'll be trying to help the mom-to-be manage the shock and the fear that she is feeling. Basically, the father is already working on two things: managing his own emotions and helping you with yours. For that reason, play down the shock when you tell him the news. Let him absorb what's happening before assaulting him with all of your fears and concerns. Focus on the joy and not the shock. At least for one day, that is.

Understand His Perspective

While you're thinking of your babies' health, how your body will change, and whether you'll be able to manage to stay awake all night for three months on end, your partner is thinking about your health, finances, the loss of his social life, and the death of his sex life. You are both worried, but about different issues, and it pays to understand his perspective.

WHAT HE'S MOST WORRIED ABOUT

Your Health

If, like me, you happened to find out you were having twins because of some health issue, like spotting or bleeding, then your partner is immediately concerned about your health. His first questions will run along the lines of "Are you okay?" and "Will you be healthy?" before he even thinks about the babies.

Your Finances

Your husband or partner will also be worried about finances and how you will both be able to support this new, larger-than-expected family, especially given the possibility that you will be on bed rest, that your family will have to depend on one income, and that you may have to shell out for a nanny to help care for your babies.

His Social Life

No matter how much you've wanted children, you can't help but worry to some degree that your social life will end once you have kids. Of course, this concern pales if you've tried for a long time to get pregnant or have battled health issues, but the shift from a lifestyle where you have the freedom, time, and energy to do the things you want to do when you want to do them to a lifestyle that revolves around your babies' sleep schedule is tough for everyone. With twins, your social life is pretty much a goner for months on end, and your husband or partner knows this. He is sad, worried, and possibly resentful, and this is *before* the babies are born.

His Sex Life

Sex during pregnancy can be great, but with a multiple pregnancy your doctor may advise you to abstain from it in the latter months. Or you may feel too uncomfortable and too tired to have sex. After the babies are born, squeezing in sex may feel like just one more chore you have to do before you can get some sleep. On the other hand, your husband or partner may be thinking that sex is the greatest thing ever, and he won't want to kiss it good-bye for the next six months. The thought of how the babies will affect his sex life will weigh pretty heavily on his mind.

Your Expectations

Conversations about parenting should probably come before pregnancy, but if they haven't, they should happen as soon as you learn you're having twins. How will you handle the pregnancy? If you're the mom-to-be, do you expect the father to come with you to doctor's appointments, or take twelve weeks off of work when the babies are born? If you're the dad-to-be, do you expect your wife or partner to take the lead in all things baby-related? Do you expect to continue your hobbies when the babies are born? These are all things to be resolved up front, in the first few weeks of pregnancy. A friend, the father of twins, told me that he wished he and his wife had discussed not only pregnancy-related issues, but also how they would divide the babies' feedings, sleep schedule, and care once they were born. As it happened, his wife had complications following her C-section delivery of their boys, so he ended up doing everything for the babies and their older son for the first two or three weeks after her delivery. Resolving their day-to-day responsibilities is still something he wishes they resolved early on.

Arranging Time Off from Work

Your husband or partner knows he will be needed at home and will already be thinking about how much time off he can get from work. It's not that he necessarily prefers to be at work (although, given the demand of infants, he's probably secretly glad that he can use work as an excuse to get back to a regular schedule and healthy dose of adult interaction as soon as possible), but he knows he will have a tough time arranging the time off. The unfortunate truth is that in our culture, outside of the most progressive workplaces, men who take too much time off are stigmatized and may even be penalized. When you tell him the news that you're having twins, he may immediately begin counting up vacation and sick days.

Formulating a Plan

More formalized than a simple discussion or series of discussions, the plan you create should outline how much time each of you will take off, how you will cover any missing income, how you will handle any medical emergencies (either yours or the babies' needs), and who is responsible for what in the first few weeks after the babies are born. Even if the plan gets adjusted over the course of the pregnancy, at least you will have a starting point for how things might play out.

DURING PREGNANCY

Pregnancy is a critical time to build parenting confidence. Use the time to practice the skills you will both need when the babies arrive. These strategies will help dads-to-be become confident and capable parents.

Take a Class

Although I mentioned it in Chapter 1, I am repeating it here: Fathers-to-be should absolutely take a specialized multiples pregnancy class. The class will cover everything from labor and delivery (sometimes pretty graphically) to basic childcare tasks, such as swaddling, diaper changing, and bathing, and it will familiarize you with the hospital's layout so that you're familiar with what the delivery process and the environment will be. Moreover, just by attending a class at the hospital, you will know exactly where to drive and park when your wife or partner is in labor and time is critical.

Become CPR-Skilled

One of the basic worries of fathers-to-be is that they won't know what to do if something goes wrong with the babies. Take a CPR class at the hospital to learn what to do in case of emergency.

Arrange Finances, Insurance, and Wills

Making sure that everything is in order with your finances now and in case of your death will give you peace of mind. During my pregnancy, my husband was obsessed with how we would be able to support ourselves, save for our children, and protect them should anything happen to us. I let him take the lead on all things related to finances, insurance, and arranging our wills, not because I didn't want to be involved or didn't think it was my place (I'm pretty opinionated about everything, including how to handle our money), but because I knew he was really concerned about these aspects of our family life and taking action would help him manage his anxiety.

Divide the Research

With so much to learn about having twins and about parenting in general, many women spend their entire pregnancies focused on researching the best products, resources, and strategies. But there's no reason this work should solely be the woman's focus. If he hasn't expressed an interest in any child-related topics, assign your husband or partner specific things to learn about. The very process of gathering information will make him more confident and more invested in the parenting process. Although your spouse may not be interested in finding the perfect décor for the babies' room or the best diaper bag, he is likely to be interested in learning about health- and safety-related issues, as well as anything that has a significant dollar amount attached to it. Think about having your partner research the following: pediatricians, cars and car seats, cribs and baby furniture, strollers, and insurance plans. Then discuss and decide together.

Prepare the Room

Getting the babies' room and furniture ready is a project most men take on, if only because, unlike a hugely pregnant woman, they have an easier time with the physical chores of painting the room, putting together the cribs, and moving furniture into place. In addition, this task lets the dad play a central role in his changing household.

Arrange the Work Schedule

Dads-to-be should check out their leave policies and talk to their bosses and human resources departments about managing their time off and work schedules. Parents of twins need to think about flexibility. Moms of twins are likely to go on bed rest during pregnancy, and both partners need to be able to accommodate an unpredictable work schedule before and after the babies are born. In addition, if your babies are born with health problems, it will mean extra time spent at the hospital or the doctor's office. If the babies are born via C-section, the dad may have to be the primary caregiver for the first couple of weeks, and that means there'll be no sleep at night. Even if the babies are healthy, dads may have to take extra time off to accompany them to their regular pediatric appointments.

Take Advantage of Time Off

Pregnancy is the last bastion of free time. This is the time to go away for a weekend, go out to dinner, or see a movie without worrying. My husband

and I made a point to go out to a New Year's Eve party while I was thirty-five weeks pregnant, just four days before I gave birth. I honestly didn't feel like going out to a party but I knew it would be my last chance to spend in the company of adults and my husband for a long time. So I went for it.

Max Out "Guy Time"

If you're the dad-to-be, pregnancy is also the time to max out your guy time. If possible, go away for that guys' weekend. Spend some extra time working out or practicing with your band, or enjoying whatever your hobby is. The key is to get your fill of your friendships now, to carry you through that long dry spell when the only people you interact with cry, sleep, and poop 24/7.

HANDS-ON TRAINING

There's nothing like actually doing something to make you confident that you can handle it. Success breeds confidence. In that spirit, let your husband or partner actually practice some of the tasks that will be coming up after the babies are born.

Pack the Diaper Bag

Getting out of the house is tough with two babies, and it becomes next to impossible if you're the only one getting the kids and all the supplies ready to go. This is why I always looked so disheveled when I left the house with the babies. After getting everyone else together, there was no time left for me. My husband always hung back and let me pack the diaper bag and get the formula ready because I was the "expert." Eliminate that argument by having your husband or partner prepare the diaper bag. Let him practice first, and then make it the real deal. There'll be no more excuses that he doesn't know what you pack or what needs to be in the bag when he's the one doing the packing.

Put Away Supplies

When buying all that baby stuff, have your husband or partner put it all away and store it. Then if you ask him to get you something, he knows where it is. It's also a way of having him monitor whether you have enough diapers, wipes, or formula on hand.

Buy and Prepare Formula

Even if you plan to breast-feed, give the dad-to-be a confidence boost by having him prepare bottles and formula. If you end up having to supplement, or supplement with breast milk in bottles, he'll be prepared. He'll need to know the parts of a bottle, how to mix the formula, and how to properly heat it up. If you know you'll be bottle-feeding, have him practice making formula in batches, too. Have him buy formula as well, so he knows exactly which brand and size you will use.

Fold and Unfold the Stroller

It looks so simple in the store, but putting together, folding, and unfolding your stroller is an exercise in frustration. I remember my husband got all bent out of shape by our strollers when we first tried to take the babies out for a walk. Inevitably, the person who uses the stroller the most becomes the expert. Ensure some equality and forestall frustration by making sure that your husband or partner becomes intimately familiar with the levers that set the brakes, collapse the stroller, attach the hood, and all of the other mysterious parts of the giant contraption that will have to be carted everywhere for the next two years.

Install and Uninstall the Car Seats

You'll need to install the car seats before you can even take the babies home from the hospital. Have your spouse practice how to install and uninstall them, especially if you need to move the car seats between two cars; how to install extra bases; and how to snap the car seats into the stroller. Installing the car seats at least once before you head for the hospital is adequate preparation, but it's better to improve his skills (and yours, for that matter) by doing multiple run-throughs.

Strap in the Babies

If you think installing and mastering the car seats is the hard part, you're wrong. It's strapping in the babies that trips everyone up! It's difficult to practice strapping in an infant or two before your babies are born, which is why dolls come in handy. Buy or borrow a couple of dolls and practice actually strapping them into the car seat. You may think this is overkill, but there's a lot to be said for knowing where the straps go and how to adjust them before you're faced with putting two tiny, crying babies into an intimidating car seat.

AFTER THE BABIES ARE BORN

The best way to keep the dad involved is to depend on him to care for the babies. Once he gets some practice, let him be the primary caregiver for part of every day.

Devise a Schedule

Parents of twins know that preparation and scheduling are the keys to keeping everything manageable. Devise a schedule that includes both partners so that one person isn't left to do all of the feeding, diaper changing, bathing, and so forth. The schedule should be organized around the babies' needs, but it should also account for times when both parents are home and include the chores you need or would like to get done, like cooking and laundry.

Take Nighttime Shifts

The best tip, both in terms of keeping the dad involved in parenting the twins and ensuring you can manage the nighttime baby feedings, is to split up the work so that each parent is in charge for a given period of time. A shift system also allows each person to get an unbroken period of five or six hours of sleep. Being the primary caregiver ensures competency. So, if the dad is the primary caregiver, even if only for a period of a few hours at night, then he maintains the skills and confidence to take care of both babies alone.

Leave Him Alone with the Babies

Yes, alone, even if it's only for two or three hours. Not only will it give the dad a sense of how much work is actually involved in caring for two babies, but it will give the mom a break from the incessant work of caring for two babies. Plus, time alone will help the father bond with the babies.

Give Him Time Off

Moms of twins know how important it is to get a break from baby-related work. But break time applies to dads, too. Even if your husband or partner has gone back to work and does not do nearly as much baby-related work as you do, it's still important to give him some time to himself, whether it's to go to the gym to blow off some steam or meet up with his friends once a week. A happy partner is a productive partner. If your spouse gets a break from helping with the babies, then when it's his turn to take over, he's not burned out and resentful. By that same token, don't immediately hand off one of the babies when your husband walks in the door from work. Give him fifteen or twenty minutes to decompress and then hand off the babies while you take a long break.

PART TWO

MANAGING THE BASICS

7

Getting Through the Night

N ight feedings, for the uninitiated, are a special form of torture for the new parent. Just as you fall asleep, you're jarred awake by a baby crying. This torment is repeated every two or three hours every night for what seems like infinity—or for about three months. The nights with my oldest daughter, whom I breast-fed, were so exhausting that I hallucinated on more than one occasion: Was I falling asleep or waking up? Why wasn't my baby in my arms? Was she under the covers? When I learned I was having twins, I was terrified of the sleep deprivation. Fortunately, my imagination was a lot worse than reality.

In the highs and lows of new parenthood, getting up from a dead sleep to soothe a shrieking baby is definitely one of the lows. Not only do you crave sleep like it's the world's greatest drug, but your baby sounds like she will wake up the neighborhood. With twins it's even worse because one baby's cries can wake up the second baby, and how on earth will you take care of both?

It's ironic, but the bright side of nighttime feedings is that you soon get used to multiple wakings and become adept at feeding, changing, and soothing the babies back to sleep. But until you get to that expert stage, there are plenty of tricks you can use to make the nights easier to bear. They fall into three general categories: dressing your babies for ease and speed (yours), creating and maintaining the optimal sleep environment, and preparing and keeping handy anything you might need to take care of your babies. If "location, location, location" is the mantra in real estate, then "preparation, preparation, preparation" is the mantra for parents of twins. Try these tips.

Immediately

✓ Turn on the faucet.

✓ Swaddle.

✓ Don't make eye contact with your baby.

✓ Heat bottles simultaneously, even if only one baby is awake.

✓ Use rolled-up receiving blankets as bottle props.

✓ Use pillows to support the babies side-by-side.

✓ Turn off the lights, even the nightlight.

✓ Put your babies down slowly and carefully.

In the Future

✓ Dress your babies in pajamas with zippers, not snaps.

✓ Alternatively, use baby gowns instead of footed pajamas.

✓ Slather on the diaper cream.

✓ Use a diaper one size larger to keep your babies drier.

✓ If bottle-feeding, store food close to where you will feed your babies.

✓ Keep a minifridge or an insulated bag with ice packs in the babies' room.

✓ Stage everything you may need during a feeding.

✓ Keep a digital clock in the babies' room.

✓ Have multiple baby and adult sleeping areas.

✓ Work in shifts.

PREPARING THE BABIES FOR BED

Believe it or not, basics like dressing, diapering, and swaddling your babies can make a huge difference in how quickly you can manage their nighttime awakenings.

Buy Pajamas with Zippers, Not Snaps

Dealing with snaps may seem easy during the day, but try doing it in the dark, when you need to change a sleepy baby as quickly as possible and with a minimum of disruption while you are barely awake. Too often, I'd manage to wake one of my twins while fumbling with their pajama snaps and set myself up for an extra twenty or thirty minutes of rocking and soothing. And when one baby is awake and crying, the second isn't too far behind.

Alternatively, Try Baby Gowns That Open at the Bottom

Some parents swear by baby gowns that open at the bottom, because all you have to do is pull them up to change the baby. I happened not to like them, because my kids wiggled so much the gowns tended to bunch up and seemed to make them uncomfortable or, alternatively, they would leave their skinny little legs exposed in a cold room. But my coworker Suzanna was so thrilled with the ease of baby gowns that she used nothing else for her twins.

Slather on the Diaper Cream

After about eight or ten weeks, once your babies are no longer peeing or pooping after every feeding (which happens more quickly for bottle-fed babies and takes longer for breast-fed babies), slather on the diaper cream and eliminate nighttime diaper changes. Your babies will be considerably calmer and sleepier if they're fed but not changed, and you can sleep longer because the feedings and nighttime disruptions will be shorter. In addition, using diaper cream will prevent diaper rash.

Try Using a Diaper One Size Larger

If your babies' diapers are always sopping wet in the mornings and you're afraid that you absolutely have to change them in the middle of the night, try using a diaper one size larger to keep babies drier. I've also had a couple of people tell me that they doubled up the diapers—two per bottom, in other words.

Swaddle Your Baby Tightly

I can't say enough about this tip. Swaddling is like a miracle cure in that it seems to calm the fussiest baby. The accepted wisdom among many new parents seems to be that babies want to be free and unwrapped shortly after coming home from the hospital. But the experience of the majority of parents interviewed for this book is that babies like to be swaddled until they are three, four, or even six months old. The general idea is to wrap the babies up tightly, so their arms and legs don't flail, replicating the crowded environment of the womb. Swaddling twins also enables one person to lift and hold both babies simultaneously. I was able to do this trick until my babies were more than eight weeks old, and they were born at healthy weights of more than five pounds for one and six-and-a-half pounds for the other. If one of your babies wakes up after having been fed, try rewrapping the baby and see if he or she doesn't go right back to sleep. There is one thing to keep in mind: Within a few days of coming home, babies seem to outgrow the receiving blankets that are typically used for swaddling them. We ended up first buying, then sewing together, larger blankets that were big enough to swaddle our growing babies.

CREATING THE OPTIMAL SLEEP ENVIRONMENT

Just like adults, babies benefit from a quiet, dark, and restful sleep environment.

Turn Off the Lights, Even the Night-Light

Lots of sleep experts recommend that parents keep the lights off as much as possible at night. It really works. We started out using a night-light but turned that off as well when the babies were a couple of months old. I found that the babies soothed themselves to sleep better and fell back asleep after feedings more quickly when the room was darker.

Don't Make Eye Contact

When holding and rocking your babies at night, don't make eye contact. It revs them up. Babies love to look at faces, and if they lock eyes with you they're more likely to fight to stay awake.

Put Your Baby Down in the Crib Slowly and Carefully

The real trick here is to move smoothly, slowly, and gently, taking extra time to shift from one movement, which is rocking the baby, to the next, which is setting the baby down. This may seem like an overly obvious step, but it's critical, and all too often it's done too hastily, with the end-result being that the babies wake up before they're even completely lying down. Imagine yourself rocking, then stopping, then laying the baby down, all in super-slow motion—that's about the pace you'll need to keep. Make sure you are touching your babies until the very final moments, when they're lying in the crib; just feeling the light pressure of your hand may be enough to prevent them from arousing.

GETTING EVERYTHING ALL READY

For a parent, being jarred awake after only an hour's sleep is bad enough, but it gets even worse when you have to stumble around in the dark to find things—from bottles and formula to pillows and blankets, and even your eyeglasses. That's why you'll want to prep everything ahead of time.

If Using Bottles, Store the Food Close to Where You Will Feed Your Babies

A dresser, hallway, or even a nearby bathroom are good places to store food for your babies if you're still using bottles. Prepare the bottles ahead of time and heat them in a bottle warmer or in warm water. The fewer steps, the less chance there is of waking up the other baby, an older child, or even that second parent.

Stage Everything

Think you'll be thirsty and want some water? Do you need your glasses to see clearly? What about some tissues or wipes? Do you need a bathrobe or a blanket if you're going to be up for thirty minutes? If you keep everything in the spot where you do your nighttime feedings, you'll eliminate the time, extra effort, and potential noise involved in having to get them. I learned to leave my eyeglasses by the bottles of formula rather than on the nightstand by my bed. I could find my way to the baby's room easily without them, and leaving them on the nightstand only meant I fumbled loudly in the dark whenever the babies' cries woke me up from a dead sleep.

Heat Two Bottles Simultaneously

If you don't want to invest in two bottle warmers, try using a bottle warmer for one and heating up the other in a sink (or oversize mug) filled with hot water. This method also works well if you're feeding one baby who eats a lot (so the baby is drinking from one bottle while the other bottle heats up).

Keep a Minifridge or Insulated Bag with Ice Packs Nearby for Nighttime Feedings

Keeping a minifridge or an insulated bag with ice packs close by is a tip we got from some friends, and, boy, did it help. Our babies' room was upstairs, but our kitchen was downstairs. Running up and down the stairs in the middle of the night was not an agreeable option. I bought a couple of insulated lunch bags, got plenty of plastic ice packs (in the free diaper bags my OB and the hospital gave me), and kept premade food in the bathroom next to the babies' bedroom. Another friend used a minifridge to keep premade food in the babies' room.

Turn on the Faucet

All three of my kids would fall asleep within five minutes after listening to the sound of running water, sometimes in the kitchen, sometimes in the bathroom. When combined with steady rocking and swaddling, turning on the faucet was foolproof time and time again.

Use Rolled-Up Receiving Blankets as Bottle Props

Most parents of singletons can't imagine propping a bottle in a baby's mouth; for parents of twins, it's virtually a necessity. I'm not advocating propping a bottle into the mouth of a baby who's lying down (it promotes ear infections) or propping up the bottle in order to be able to go back to sleep. Instead, use bottle props when you need to begin feeding one baby in order to pick up the other. When both babies are side-by-side, you can feed them simultaneously. Make use of the giant inventory of receiving blankets you bought or received for your shower and that the babies outgrew after one week. Folded and rolled, they make excellent and convenient bottle props.

Use Pillows to Support the Babies Side-by-Side

One person can feed both babies by laying them side-by-side on the floor, with their heads supported by firm pillows. (We used a Boppy and another maternity pillow that I received as a gift, both of which we stored under the babies' cribs for easy access.) Although I didn't discover this trick until well in the game (probably month two), I made use of it many times afterward!

Keep a Digital Clock in the Babies' Room

A clock you can easily see will help you monitor the length and frequency of feedings and orient you in the middle of the night. A digital clock can also be used to convince your spouse that you did more work, because you can say, "Honey, I was up for an hour the last feeding. Now it's your turn."

Have Multiple Baby and Adult Sleeping Areas

For the first few weeks, many babies feel more secure in bassinets than they do in cribs. If you keep two bassinets (or two Pack 'n Plays, for instance) in a room other than the babies' bedroom or your own bedroom, it gives you many more options for staging nighttime feedings, for separating a crying baby from a sleeping one, and for separating a sleeping parent from crying babies in those harrowing first few weeks. For instance, if you have a house where the bedrooms are on a different level than the living room, you can have two bassinets in the living room so you can feed the babies and put them to sleep and then be able to watch TV or sleep on the sofa. Meanwhile, upstairs, the other parent is blissfully asleep, until his shift begins.

Work in Shifts

Virtually all of the parents I've spoken with have talked about teaming up to manage nighttime feedings and wakings. One couple whose babies tended to wake each other decided to split them up, especially because one baby was fussier than the other. At night, the adults slept separately, each with a baby in a bassinet next to them. The couple alternated nights with the fussier baby so that one person did not have to bear the brunt of the longer feedings and wakings. This arrangement lasted three months, which seems about average for major nighttime wakings for many babies. And frankly, it's a small price to pay for the extra sleep and peace of mind. In our household, after two nights of taking turns getting out of bed to feed the babies, we instituted a nightly shift system. I took the 8:00 p.m. to 2:00 a.m. shift, while my husband took the 2:00 a.m. to 8:00 a.m. shift. The beauty of this system was that each of us got roughly five to six hours of unbroken sleep each night.

8

Breast-Feeding

As someone who experienced success with breast-feeding when I had my first child, I really wanted to breast-feed my twins, but I was bewildered and apprehensive about the process. I couldn't quite visualize how I might breast-feed two babies. Wouldn't one baby fall off? And how would I be able to lift one baby so that the other did not fall off my breast? Did breast-feeding twins require two people, one to nurse them and the other to lift them up or off? The more I thought about it, the more worried I became. And frankly, my experience with the hospital's lactation consultant was not at all positive. She made me feel inadequate in my attempts to breast-feed in the hospital and flat out told me that breast-feeding twins alone at home was not possible for at least the first few weeks. But in my situation, it was not realistic to have someone help me with nursing the twins. I left the hospital with limited skills and feeling undermined. Sadly, the lactation consultant was right—I wasn't able to do it alone, and after six weeks of trying I gave up. But I also made it a mission when doing research for this book to learn from people who were successful at breast-feeding their twins. And what I learned is this: You need to feel positive and optimistic about your ability to do it, but you also need to get informed; to practice when possible; to be perseverant and learn practical strategies, such as how to lift and position the babies; and to have the appropriate supplies. Here are some suggestions.

Building Your Confidence
✓ Get expert help.
✓ Prescreen lactation consultants.

✓ Find out if your insurance covers a lactation consultant.

✓ Tap your twins network.

✓ Contact twins forums.

✓ Educate your spouse or partner.

✓ Practice in the hospital.

✓ Educate yourself so you don't feel pressured to bottle-feed.

✓ Expect some setbacks.

✓ Don't beat yourself up.

✓ Set short-term goals.

✓ Prepare yourself to go 23/7.

✓ Give yourself time to decide whether to use a pump.

✓ Have help on speed dial.

✓ Feel good about your choices.

Having the Right Supplies

✓ Buy a nursing pillow designed for twins.

✓ Test-drive nursing pillows.

✓ Buy extra pillows.

✓ Get a daybed.

✓ Enlist your spouse or partner.

✓ Get a hospital-grade breast pump.

Adopting a Step-by-Step Process for Nursing

✓ Find a place to spread out.

✓ Stage everything.

✓ Go to the bathroom.

✓ Put your babies on Boppies.

✓ Surround yourself with pillows.

✓ Start with one baby first.

✓ Position the first baby.

✓ Help your baby latch on.

✓ Position the second baby.

✓ Lean back.

✓ Burp each baby.

✓ Put each baby down.

Important Things to Keep in Mind

✓ Switch the babies (alternate breasts) periodically.

✓ Observe whether one baby may be a better or more aggressive nurser.

✓ Keep a breast-feeding log.

If You Encounter Problems

✓ Try a supplemental nursing system.

✓ Use a pump to keep up your milk supply.

✓ Try fenugreek.

✓ Sleep more.

✓ Nourish yourself.

✓ Try nonalcoholic beer.

✓ Eat oats, barley, or kasha.

✓ Don't use nipple shields.

✓ Avoid medications that decrease milk supply.

BUILDING YOUR CONFIDENCE

The best way to ensure a successful breast-feeding experience is to start with information and support. Then, even if your confidence wanes if you encounter difficulties in the process, you can regroup and try again.

Get Expert Help

Expert help can be a godsend. A lactation consultant will teach you how to breast-feed your babies, including how to position them and get them to latch on to your breast. They are the breast-feeding experts, and you can get referrals from your OB or midwife, as well as your hospital. You can also contact La Leche League (www.llli.org) or check out the International Lactation Consultant Association (www.ilca.org) or the International Board of Lactation Consultant Examiners (www.iblce.org) online to get names of local lactation consultants.

Prescreen Lactation Consultants

In my situation, I think it would have been helpful if I'd contacted a lactation consultant before my babies were born. This would have given me a chance to establish a rapport with her and figure out if her personality and approach to breast-feeding were compatible with mine. As it was, I happened to work with a lactation consultant whom I found abrasive and unhelpful, which greatly colored my overall experience.

Find Out If Your Insurance Covers a Lactation Consultant

Getting expert help can be expensive. Check to see if your insurer will cover the cost and, if so, under what circumstances those costs will be covered.

Tap Your Twins Network

If you belong to a twins or multiples club, you have a ready resource of other mothers of twins, many with direct experience in breast-feeding their babies. But the trick, of course, is to join the club *before* you give birth so that you are armed with names and phones numbers before you're desperate for them. That said, other moms of twins can offer support for as long as you nurse, not just in the first few weeks, so it's never too late to call for advice.

Contact Twins Forums

The next best thing to an in-person visit or a phone call in middle of the night is to "talk" to someone over the Internet. Many twins forums, including www.twinstuff.com, have discussion threads on breast-feeding twins, and the moms online can be a tremendous resource, or at least a virtual shoulder to cry on.

Educate Your Spouse or Partner

Successful breast-feeding requires a lot of emotional and sometimes physical support. Spouses or partners will be more supportive if they are fully on-board with the plan to breast-feed. The best way to get them there, of course, is to educate them about the benefits and challenges of breast-feeding twins. Even though there is much more awareness and acceptance of breast-feeding today than there was just a few years ago, you may still encounter a lot of skepticism about breast-feeding, especially with twins. A supportive partner can help run interference with critics and can also actively participate in the breast-feeding process (by handing you the babies or helping you position them, for example).

Practice in the Hospital

Your best opportunity to get instruction and training in the art of breast-feeding with real live babies (as opposed to just the dolls used in breast-feeding classes) is while you are in the hospital. Seek out the hospital's lactation consultant and keep trying to nurse while you're there. Colostrum, also known as "first milk," comes in within days of giving birth and your babies may get some while you are still in the hospital. Research shows that babies, especially premature babies, benefit from colostrum.

Educate Yourself So You Don't Feel Pressured to Bottle-Feed

While you may enter the hospital fully committed to breast-feeding, you may leave with two babies who are bottle-fed. And you may not even fully understand how it happened, because in the craziness of the delivery and in the moments—or even days—*after* your twins are born, you aren't thinking about what you decided in that vacuum of time before your babies were born, you're thinking about what's best for them now that they're here. In most circumstances, the hospital will tell you that bottle-feeding is necessary for the health and well-being of your babies, especially if they're premature. That's exactly what happened to me, as well as many of the women I spoke with. We were told to give the twins formula because they needed to gain weight quickly, and we dutifully did so. But to this day, three years later, I wonder if I should have pressed on with breast-feeding. I chalk it up to my lack of knowledge and my lazy assurance that because I nursed my older daughter I could "wing it" with the twins. It's with hindsight that I say, learn what you can about breast-feeding, especially in regard to preemies, so that if you're faced with nurses or physicians who are pressuring you to bottle-feed your babies, you can make an educated decision either way.

Expect Some Setbacks

Like everything related to child rearing, breast-feeding may not go exactly as you anticipated and you may encounter some problems and frustrations, both initially and over time. For instance, you may have trouble getting one or both of your babies to latch on to your breast, or you may have problems with your milk supply. The key is not to romanticize the experience to the point where the first problem you encounter throws you into a tailspin and you give up entirely.

Don't Beat Yourself Up

As mothers, we have a tendency to blame ourselves when things don't go as we hope or want for our children. If you find you're having problems with breast-feeding, there's no point in beating yourself up about it. Accept that you're having some issues and work to ensure that your babies are getting the best nutrition possible, even if it's formula.

Set Short-Term Goals

In the beginning, it's easy to envision a long, beautiful experience with nursing. You may think you'll breast-feed for six months, a year, or three years. But you'll do yourself a favor if you simply take it step-by-step. Set short-term goals, such as committing to breast-feeding for two weeks and then reassessing where you are after that time. If after two weeks things are going well, then recommit for another two weeks or for a month. But setting out with a long-term goal can undermine your progress, because during the sleepless nights, when your babies are having trouble latching on and you're about to cry from exhaustion and frustration, even six months can seem like an eternity. It's easy to give up when faced with an interminable problem that seems unsolvable.

Prepare Yourself to Go 23/7

Breast-feeding is enormously time-consuming initially. Each baby needs to be fed every two or three hours, and some babies can take twenty, thirty, or even forty minutes at each feeding. Basically, all you'll be doing for the first few days is nursing your twins, with maybe an hour or two for sleep. But then, once everybody gets the hang of it, the feedings get shorter. The babies learn to latch on and become efficient nursers, and you and your partner learn how best to handle and position the twins. Keep that in mind in those first few sleepless nights.

Give Yourself Time to Decide Whether to Use a Pump

For women who want to breast-feed, expressing breast milk by using a pump represents some freedom. With a decent supply of expressed breast milk on hand, you can hand over some of the feedings to the dad or feel better about returning to work. But building a supply is a tough process. Many moms purchase or rent a breast pump and proceed with both nursing and pumping, but soon they work themselves into a state of sheer exhaustion. Because infants nurse so frequently, there's barely enough time to nurse them, even without the added pressure of pumping. In the weeks after their birth, I would nurse the twins, then pump for an additional twenty minutes or more. That meant I was nursing or pumping for an hour at every single feeding! A friend of mine, whose twins were born a couple of months prematurely and were hospitalized for weeks, exhausted herself pumping every two hours, even getting up in the middle of the night to pump. No matter how much you want to build up a milk supply, don't attempt to do it all only to find yourself overcome by the labor involved. If possible, delay pumping until your twins are efficient nursers and on a reasonable and stable schedule.

Have Help on Speed Dial

Keep a list of phone numbers for lactation consultants and nursing buddies and keep it handy, right by the phone, if possible. Similarly, bookmark the websites with good nursing information so that you can get to those online resources or forums quickly. This way your spouse or partner has access to the same information or can make calls on your behalf.

Feel Good About Your Choices

If you'd like to breast-feed but can't, or if you try to breast-feed but aren't successful, or if you simply decide that breast-feeding will not work for you, feel good that you made the right decision for your family and your babies. Breast-feeding to exhaustion is not going to make you healthy, and being physically unable to breast-feed is not going to scar your children emotionally.

HAVING THE RIGHT SUPPLIES

Breast-feeding twins may be daunting, but it is possible, especially if you have the right tools.

Buy a Nursing Pillow Designed for Twins
Regular nursing pillows are not big enough to comfortably support two babies. One popular brand is the EZ-2-Nurse pillow, which is a large, inflatable U-shaped pillow with wide supports for the babies. Many moms swear by it.

Test-Drive Nursing Pillows
Nursing pillows can be quite expensive, easily around $50 each. And even if a particular pillow is highly recommended, remember that not every brand works for every woman. For example, women who are on the tall and slender side may have problems with the fit of the wildly popular EZ-2-Nurse pillow, which tends to gap, making it difficult to feel like you have a secure fit. We ended up not using the pillow we bought because it just did not work for us. To avoid a costly mistake, test-drive the pillows before buying. Often, instructors of multiples pregnancy classes (or breast-feeding classes) have different brands that you can try out.

Buy Extra Pillows
Even with a nursing pillow, you may need extra support for your back or around your hips. Regular pillows are fine, but sofa pillows and floor pillows are even better. Have at least eight to ten, or even a dozen, pillows on hand.

Get a Daybed
Rockers and gliders are popular with parents-to-be. And who wouldn't want to sit in a comfy chair rocking or gliding her baby to sleep? Moms of twins, that's who. A standard-size rocker or glider is simply not big enough to hold both babies. You will not be able to nurse both babies at the same time. Buy an oversize chair or, even better, a daybed so that you can spread out, have extra pillows around you, or sit cross-legged if you want to. You'll even be able to sleep comfortably in the twins' room, if necessary.

Enlist Your Spouse or Partner

Until you get the hang of things, have your spouse help with the logistics of nursing the first few times. Have him hand you the babies one by one while you work on learning to hold them properly and getting them to latch on.

Get a Hospital-Grade Breast Pump

If you do plan to pump, rent a hospital-grade machine to make the pumping sessions as quick and efficient as possible.

ADOPTING A STEP-BY-STEP PROCESS FOR NURSING

Here's a step-by-step breakdown of how to nurse your twins. The recommendations are compiled from moms who've "been there, done that."

Find a Place to Spread Out

The sofa is an ideal place to nurse your twins, as is the floor. You want somewhere where you can spread out all of your pillows and assorted other items but still have them within arm's reach. Save the oversize chair for when you're an old hand at nursing.

Stage Everything

Before you even begin feeding your babies, make sure you have everything you might need: pillows, nursing pillow, blankets or burp cloths, a watch or clock, water, tissues, eyeglasses, TV remote, telephone, Boppy pillows, and vibrating chairs or car seats. If you have an older child or children, make sure they have everything they need (a snack, a drink) and are comfortable as well.

Go to the Bathroom

It may seem obvious, when you're reading this, but try holding off going to the bathroom for twenty or forty minutes. It gets *very* uncomfortable.

Put Your Babies on Boppies

Once you've staged everything, bring your babies close to you, ideally at the level of your hips so that you can easily bend over and lift them up. A Boppy pillow works great for this maneuver, but so will a vibrating chair if it's on a level surface, such as a coffee table or the floor. A car seat works on a level surface, too, but usually car seats are quite a bit deeper and you may have trouble reaching in and getting your hand under the babies if they're curled, as they are in a deeper seat. Remember, you will probably be lifting the baby with one hand and using the other mainly as support, so the flatter position works better.

Surround Yourself with Pillows

Put the nursing pillow around you, then support yourself with other pillows. Put them behind your back, as well as one on each side of you. Make yourself as comfortable as possible. You definitely want pillows immediately around you in case you need to rest one of the babies there before or after you put the baby to your breast.

Start with One Baby First

For the initial feedings, feed one baby after the other. That way you can practice having the babies latch on, plus you will get practice lifting your baby from the seated position.

Position the First Baby

There are several common nursing holds. The clutch or football hold is when you tuck a baby under each arm; the cradle is when the baby's head is in the crook of your elbow; and the side-by-side or parallel hold is when one baby is in the crook of your elbow while the other lays a bit lower, with the baby's head on the other's tummy. Or you can do a combo, where one baby is in the cradle position while the other is in a football hold.

Help Your Baby Latch On

After the baby is in position, help her latch on. The baby should grasp your entire nipple in her mouth. Alternatively, you can try positioning the second baby, then trying to get both to latch on. Personally, I found it easier to get one baby going before even attempting the second baby.

Position the Second Baby

Now it gets tricky. For the first few feedings, you can have your husband or partner hand you the second baby so that you can position him and help him latch on. But if you're on your own, you will have to gently lean over with one baby latched on and lift the second baby. This is why having sofa pillows and Boppy pillows all around you is so important. Twins may be born at smaller birth weights, but they're still difficult to lift with one hand, if only because you're nervous or trying to be extra careful in order not to disturb the first baby. I tended to hunch over a bit more and used the crook of my elbow to help keep Baby A in place while I lifted Baby B. Still, at least half the time, Baby A would fall off the nipple and I would have to reposition her after I positioned Baby B and got him latched on. I also liked to sit so that my legs were bent at the knee and my feet were resting on the coffee table. That allowed me to lean back and support one or both of the babies nearly upright on my thighs as I tried to get them on or off of the nursing pillows. Basically I moved them in stages, first lifting them off the sofa, then putting them onto my thighs, then onto the nursing pillow, and finally latching them onto my breasts. After the feeding, I did the same process in reverse.

Lean Back

Use gravity to help you position the babies so that they are turned toward you instead of facing up. You don't want to hunch over them; they should lean toward you, almost lying on their side. You may discover that having a pillow under your knees will help you get comfortable in this position.

Burp Each Baby

When your babies are finished nursing, lift Baby A off of your breast and put him upright against your thighs (remember, you're sitting with your legs up and bent at the knee), then lift Baby B and place her upright, too. Lean forward to meet them so that both babies are against your chest and place your hands behind each baby, then lean back while supporting them. You should now be leaning back with both babies against your chest or shoulder, in the perfect position to burp them.

Put Each Baby Down

After burping them, lean forward and place both babies against your knees. Take one baby and place her in her Boppy pillow, then take the second baby and place him in his Boppy. From there, you can sit up, reposition yourself, or stand up.

IMPORTANT THINGS TO KEEP IN MIND

Once you get the hang of nursing, you still have to remember to alternate breasts and to keep a breast-feeding log.

Switch the Babies (Alternate Breasts) Periodically

You can either switch the twins at every feeding or assign one breast per baby per day. This allows each of the babies to look at you from different positions.

Observe Whether One Baby May Be a Better or More Aggressive Nurser

Here's another reason it's important to switch breasts: One breast may have a bigger milk supply if you always put your more aggressive nurser to that breast, so you may set up a situation where one baby is constantly getting more breast milk. That is what happened in my case. My son was a better nurser and preferred the breast with the bigger milk production (duh, I would too!). Because he squirmed and refused to latch on to the other breast, I tended to keep him on his "preferred" breast while my daughter got less and less breast milk and more and more formula.

Keep a Breast-Feeding Log

A log will help you track how often and for how long each baby nurses. Your pediatrician will ask you to detail their feedings to help gauge if the babies are getting enough breast milk. A chalkboard or whiteboard works great for this task, as does a regular plain old notebook.

IF YOU ENCOUNTER PROBLEMS

Many women worry they won't have enough milk to nurse both babies, but thankfully, most mothers find that it's not the case. However, if you do happen to see your milk supply diminish, here are some strategies you can try.

Try a Supplemental Nursing System

You may find it useful to try a supplemental nursing system, also known as a supplemental feeding-tube device. Essentially, this is a bottle with a cord that hangs around your neck, with some flexible plastic tubing that extends down toward your breast. You wear the bottle so it hangs between your breasts and tape the tubes on the top of your nipples. Your babies then "nurse" at the breast by latching onto both the breast and the tube. The system is supposed to stimulate the mother's milk supply by providing the baby with the motivation to suck well.

Use a Pump to Keep Up Your Milk Supply

Increase your milk supply by "dry pumping," or pumping after your milk stops flowing. Pump for about five minutes after your milk stops, in order to encourage increased milk production.

Try Fenugreek

Fenugreek is a medicinal herb that increases your milk supply, often within the first one to three days of use. It is available as a pill (considered to be more potent) or as a tea, and can be purchased at health food stores. Since this product is not safe for some women (in particular, those with asthma or diabetes), make sure you check with your doctor first before using it.

Sleep More

Being exhausted has a detrimental effect on your milk supply. Try increasing your sleep time if you notice that your milk production has diminished. It might be that you're just too tired.

Nourish Yourself

Eat more and drink more liquids to ensure you have all of the nutrients you need to stay healthy and hydrated.

Try Nonalcoholic Beer

There are many factors involved in establishing and maintaining a good milk supply, such as frequent nursing sessions and effective sucking by the babies. There is also an ingredient in beer (a polysaccharide from barley) that has been shown to increase milk supply by stimulating prolactin secretion. However, the suggestion to try nonalcoholic beer is strictly based on what other moms have tried. Alcoholic beer is obviously *not* recommended for nursing mothers, because alcohol passes through the milk and to your babies, and studies have shown that nursing babies actually consume less milk when the mother has consumed alcohol in the immediate hours before breastfeeding.

Eat Oats, Barley, or Kasha

Oatmeal, barley, and kasha all seem to help increase milk supply. Eat a bowl of oatmeal every day, or prepare and cook barley and kasha (which is like rice) and eat that every day.

Don't Use Nipple Shields

If your nipples are sore, you may want to use nipple shields to prevent the constant chafing and irritation. But by protecting your breasts, the shields also decrease stimulation to the breast. Less stimulation can lead to less milk.

Avoid Medications That Decrease Milk Supply

Antihistamines and decongestants can decrease your supply of breast milk, as can birth control pills, so avoid them.

9

Bottle-Feeding

Bottle-feeding twins is generally pretty easy, in part because more than one person can help with the babies and because once you get in the groove, you can prepare bottles quickly and easily. But it can also get expensive and messy, and many women feel they're somehow letting their babies down by choosing or being forced to bottle-feed. Here are some tips for how to bottle-feed your infant twins and how best to stock up on all the necessary supplies (saving some cash while doing it) and keep them manageable in your house.

General Considerations
✓ Decide whether to schedule.
✓ Keep track of feedings.

Formula and Supplies
✓ Don't prestock formula.
✓ Buy powdered formula to save money.
✓ Go generic if possible.
✓ Wait a month before stocking up.
✓ Purchase cases.
✓ Know the price per ounce.
✓ Buy formula online, but use caution.
✓ Keep formula coupons in your car.
✓ Buy a Crock-Pot.
✓ Build a supply of bottles, caps, nipples, and liners.
✓ Make sure your bottle caps match your bottles.

✓ Keep all the small pieces together.

✓ Get a bottle organizer.

Preparing Formula

✓ Make formula by the pitcher.

✓ Keep track of feedings by marking each baby's bottles.

✓ Differentiate bottles.

✓ Keep a bowl of sudsy water in your sink.

✓ Use the nipple brush that comes with your bottle brush.

✓ Keep the scoops that come with your formula.

Feeding the Babies

✓ Accept that you will have to use bottle props.

✓ Get the Podee "hands free" feeding system.

✓ Feed the quiet baby first.

✓ Position the babies.

✓ Swaddle the babies for feedings.

GENERAL CONSIDERATIONS

Scheduling feedings helps you manage the entire experience of parenting twins, and keeping track of them helps both you and the babies' doctor chart their growth.

Decide Whether to Schedule

Mothers of twins have to decide whether they want their babies to feed on demand or whether they should schedule their feedings. Bottle-feeding lends itself to scheduling, because it's easy to see how much your baby drinks and you can mix as much formula as you need. The benefit of scheduling feedings is that you spend less time overall feeding the babies—perhaps twenty rather than forty minutes. And if you schedule the feedings, the babies will also need to be changed and will sleep at the same times, so you can get more sleep during the night and keep your sanity. Although the decision is personal, the consensus among moms of twins is that raising twins is much more manageable if the babies are on a schedule.

Keep Track of Feedings

Write down when and how much each baby drinks, so that you can plan the next feeding and track whether your babies are eating enough. Your pediatrician will want to know this information as well.

FORMULA AND SUPPLIES

Choice and *expense* are the bywords of bottle-feeding. You have to figure out which formula, bottles, and nipples your babies will need or prefer, and then, of course, the formula is expensive. For parents of twins, there's twice the choice and twice the cost, so savings and organization are very important.

Don't Prestock Formula
You'll get an initial supply of bottled formula from the hospital, so there's no reason for you to prestock. The nursing staff is likely to send you home with a couple of cases. True, the bottles are fairly small (two ounces), but there should be enough to last you several days, if not a couple of weeks. Don't feel shy about taking them either, because it's quite likely that your insurance will be billed for these supplies regardless of whether you take them or not.

Buy Powdered Formula to Save Money
Buying powdered formula will save you money. It's considerably cheaper than ready-to-drink or prepared formula. Plus, it allows you to mix it as you need it, unlike ready-to-drink formula, which must be consumed within the time specified on the container, usually within twenty-four to forty-eight hours. Both types of formulas do need to be refrigerated: prepared formula as soon as it's opened, and powdered formula as soon as it's mixed.

Go Generic If Possible
There's really not much difference between brand-name formula and store or generic brands, since all infant formulas are regulated by the U.S. Food and Drug Administration (FDA) and must meet certain nutrition standards—so, by all means, go generic. If you're not comfortable using no-name or store brands, discuss it with your babies' doctor. When we expressed our dismay at the price of formula, our doctor assured us that we had nothing to worry about if we wanted to use generic, as long as it wasn't the absolute cheapest brand available. The FDA has some very helpful information on infant formulas, including a nutrient list and information on DHA (docosahexaenoic acid) and ARA (arachidonic acid), on its website. Check it out at www.cfsan.fda.gov/~dms/inf-faq.html.

Wait a Month Before Stocking Up
Given the expense, it's very tempting to rush out and stock up on formula by purchasing it by the case—but wait a month first. It's quite likely that your babies will need or prefer different types or brands of formula. For

example, many babies with reflux are put on soy formula. You don't want to have purchased formula you can't use.

Purchase Cases
Once you know what formula is right for your babies, it's time to think about saving money. Buy cases rather than individual containers of formula, because costs can drop dramatically as quantity increases.

Know the Price per Ounce
If you shop at discount warehouses, like Costco or Sam's Club, you're probably aware that the sizes of items sold in these stores don't correspond to the sizes sold in regular groceries or drugstores. This means you can't easily determine whether what you're paying for is a good deal unless you know the price per ounce. Memorize or jot down the per-ounce cost of the formula you use so that you can determine whether that giant container is really a value. (Surprisingly, very often it's not such a great value at all.)

Buy Formula Online, but Use Caution
Many people use websites such as eBay or Craigslist to buy and sell formula or formula coupons. Please use caution and common sense when buying formula online. Contact reliable sellers (be sure to check their reviews from previous sellers) and try to determine, to the degree possible, that you're getting what you're paying for. You definitely want to make sure that the formula is safe and not tampered with. The FDA website has information on how to detect counterfeit formula and the general things to be aware of in terms of formula safety.

Keep Formula Coupons in Your Car
Open a can of formula and you're likely to find a savings coupon either affixed under the lid or sometimes attached right on the can. Take advantage of these coupons, because they can generally save you a minimum of $2 or $3 off of the retail price. But coupons go to waste if you don't have them when you go shopping. Get a folder or a zippered pouch (or even a plastic freezer bag) to hold them and keep it in the glove compartment of your car.

Buy a Crock-Pot
A Crock-Pot is extremely handy for parents of twins for two reasons: One, it's a great alternative to a bottle warmer, and two, it makes preparing meals much easier. You can keep the Crock-Pot filled with heated water all day and just pop in bottles as you need them warmed. It's ideal for an area where you don't have access to a sink. Overall, I think a Crock-Pot is superior to a

standard bottle warmer, because bottles immersed in water seem to warm better and faster than in a regular bottle warmer, and you can warm up multiple bottles at the same time. A Crock-Pot also has a long afterlife: Once it's done serving as a bottle warmer, it can be used to prepare meals.

Build a Supply of Bottles, Caps, Nipples, and Liners

With twins, not only will you need a lot of bottles, caps, and nipples on hand, but your babies may prefer different types of bottles or nipples. Start small: Buy two different types of bottles (with liners, if necessary), and two or three different types of nipples. Then, as you discover what each baby prefers, build your supply. If you are making a two-hour trip to the store, you'll have to take two to four bottles along. It's not unusual to have to take six bottles with you on longer errands, and if you don't wash dishes promptly you'll only kick yourself when you get home and realize you have to hunt through all of your stuff for the bottles and wash them, all while your babies are wailing with hunger.

Make Sure Your Bottle Caps Match Your Bottles

Bottles of milk tend to tip over no matter how you carry or pack them— whether in your backpack, diaper bag, stroller, or insulated lunch bag. And when they leak, things get messy. Capping bottles is essential, but too often you'll find you don't have bottles and caps that are compatible. Make sure you buy enough caps and that those caps fit the bottles you use.

Keep All the Small Pieces Together

Designate a container for storing all of your bottles and bottle caps, and another to store all of your nipples. Keep them on your counter, within easy reach and preferably close to your sink, so you can just drop the items in after they're washed and dried. Many times you're so rushed trying to prepare and warm up two bottles of formula that you can't really spare the time to hunt for those elusive nipples. By having them in separate containers and out on your counter, you can easily reach in and grab what you need.

Get a Bottle Organizer

Another way to save space and keep your bottles handy is to get a bottle organizer. There are many different designs, including spinning racks, tree-like stands, and six-bottle containers that look a bit like egg cartons or milk carriers. The First Years makes a product called the 3 in 1 Feeding Organizer that can be mounted under a kitchen cabinet and is a great space-saving option. However, if you just want a bottle-drying rack, see if your dishwasher can pull double-duty before going out and spending money on a specially designed product.

PREPARING FORMULA

There are lots of ways to ease the preparation time and clean up involved in bottle-feeding. There are also a lot of great tips on how to tell which bottle belongs to which baby.

Make Formula by the Pitcher

Use a blender to quickly prepare a pitcher of formula and keep it in your refrigerator. If you're not a math whiz, keep a calculator handy in the kitchen to tally how many scoops you need for one pitcher. You can then either fill individual bottles (which, while convenient, can make your fridge crowded) or store it in a plastic pitcher and pour into bottles as needed.

Keep Track of Feedings by Marking Each Baby's Bottles

If you're pumping breast milk in addition to using formula, you want to use as much breast milk as possible and not let any go to waste. Like many women, I would express the breast milk into bottles, then cap those bottles and store them in the fridge. But for a long time, my twins did not consume a single eight-ounce bottle in a single feeding. They would drink a couple of ounces and I would have to refrigerate the remainder. After a short while, I had several bottles with varying amounts of breast milk and I was never sure which baby drank from which bottle, or how much each baby drank at any given feeding. At first I tried to keep track by putting the bottles on different shelves in the refrigerator, but confusion reigned when my husband fed the babies because he didn't pay attention to my little tracking system.

After a few days, I devised another, better system. The process sounds complicated, but was actually very simple—so simple my husband quickly got on board with it and started noting who drank what and when. I recommend this system to you:

* Before actually using the breast milk, label each bottle with the babies' initials (generally, I would write the baby's initial on a piece of clear tape that I would stick on the bottle cap). Put a second piece of tape somewhere on the bottle with the baby's initial, plus the date the breast milk was expressed, to make certain you are using the oldest milk first.
* After each feeding, grab another piece of clear tape and mark a line to

show how much milk remains in the bottle, and write down the number of ounces the baby consumed, as well as the time of the last feeding (for example, I would write something like "2.5 oz, 2:00 p.m."). When the bottle is finished, you might have three different pieces of tape at different levels, denoting different amounts and times.

* Before washing the bottle, write down all the information in a notepad, or try peeling off the pieces of tape (if you can, without tearing them) and just stick them onto the notepad.

You can simplify this system by placing a single strip of clear or masking tape vertically along the entire length of the bottle and marking the amount consumed at each feeding. The downside of this simpler system is that you can't capture nearly as much information as when using individual pieces of tape.

Differentiate Bottles

If you're not concerned about tracking each individual feeding but still need to differentiate between bottles of breast milk and formula, or between two different types of formula, you can easily do so by using a piece of tape or, alternatively, rubber bands as markers.

Keep a Bowl of Sudsy Water in Your Sink

Keep a bowl of sudsy water either in or next to your sink and just drop in bottle nipples when you're done using them. This practice will help prevent formula buildup in the crevices of the nipple. If you can fit a large bowl in the sink or on the counter, you can also immerse whole bottles so they don't get crusty before you have a chance to thoroughly wash them.

Use the Nipple Brush That Comes with Your Bottle Brush

It took me six months to realize that the handle end of my bottlebrush actually housed a specially designed nipple brush. (I blame my ignorance on not getting enough sleep, and that's the story I'm sticking to.) Use it, but remember to scrub carefully so you don't tear through the nipple tip.

Keep the Scoops That Come with Your Formula

Yes, every container comes with a new scooper, but the fine consistency of formula means that even if you get the scoop just slightly wet, the formula begins to clump immediately, making it more difficult to accurately measure out the correct amount of formula per ounce of water. As you finish each container, save the scoop and wash it out. Keep it with the bottle nipples.

FEEDING THE BABIES

Compared to breast-feeding, bottle-feeding can be easier on the parents, if only because they can share the responsibility more equally. But there are ways to make even bottle-feeding easier.

Accept That You Will Have to Use Bottle Props

You're going to have to use bottle props to some degree, most likely at night. Many moms have qualms about propping up bottles for their babies, because they think they are somehow neglecting them. But when you have two crying babies, you always feel like you are neglecting one if you are feeding or holding the other. And if you are bottle-feeding your twins at the same time, you mostly end up holding only the bottles and looking at your babies, rather than cuddling with them or holding them close. (It's very difficult to hold two infants on your lap and cradle them during feedings if they're both drinking from bottles, because your arms tend to twist awkwardly and your wrists end up hurting after a short while.) By propping up the bottle for Baby A—for example, by using a rolled-up blanket—you can then help Baby B if he needs his bottle adjusted or needs to be soothed. Bottle props, ironically, allow you to engage in more physical contact with both babies, because they leave your hands free to stroke each baby. You can also use them when you have to change one baby while feeding the other.

Get the Podee "Hands-Free" Feeding System

Some mothers of twins swear by the Podee hands-free bottle because it allows you to feed both babies at the same time. The bottle has a long flexible plastic tube that is connected to a standard nipple, the kind used in regular bottles, and the babies essentially suck the formula or milk through the long strawlike tube. A big selling point of this product is that you can feed the babies upright, which is a position that helps reduce ear infections.

Feed the Quiet Baby First

It seems counterintuitive, but if one of your twins is already crying and the other is quiet but is about to start crying (or is on the verge of waking up), feed the quiet baby first, then you'll only have one agitated infant on your hands.

Position the Babies

There are several ways to position your babies so you can feed them both. You can:

* Prop both babies on a pillow and feed them while sitting on the sofa or bed.
* Put the babies in Boppy pillows so that they're slightly angled with their heads higher up, then feed them. (An upright position also helps to prevent ear infections.)
* Sit on the floor with your legs in a V and your back against something supportive (e.g., a wall or the back of a chair), then place a baby on each thigh, or on a pillow, and feed them.

Swaddle the Babies for Feedings

Most infants like being swaddled and settle down quickly once they're all snugly wrapped. If you're having a difficult time managing both babies during feedings because they squirm or flail, try swaddling them first.

10

Bathing

While it's certainly easier to bathe twins if you have two people, one person *can* do it alone, even if you have a small bathroom. Lots of mothers, including me, have done exactly that. It's manageable if you don't let your anxiety get in the way, and if you prepare the space so that you can watch both babies at the same time. You'll also need appropriate bath supplies, including a good baby bathtub or two and some hooded towels. Then when they get bigger, your twins can bathe together while you shield yourself from all their splashing. Here are some tips.

Before Starting
✓ Accept, but don't get overwhelmed by, your anxiety.
✓ Limit your anxiety by reducing the number of baths.

Bathing Strategies
✓ Bathe the babies in the kitchen sink.
✓ Bathe the babies in the shower.
✓ Bathe the babies in other rooms.
✓ Involve two adults and split the responsibilities.
✓ Bathe with the babies.

When You Have an Older Child
✓ Involve your older child.
✓ Bathe the twins and an older child together.
✓ Distract your older child.

When You're Alone
✓ Use accessories.
✓ Use hooded towels.
✓ Undress and dress your babies in the bathroom.
✓ Warm up the water between babies.
✓ Bring in two towels for each baby.
✓ Bring in two small seats or pillows.
✓ Bring a bottle and bottle prop, just in case.
✓ Bathe them together when the twins can sit up.

Making Bath Time More Comfortable for You
✓ Protect your knees.
✓ Store towels and washcloths within easy reach.
✓ Install a faucet guard.
✓ Keep extra towels handy.

Choosing Bath Aids
✓ Get a rubber mat.
✓ Try an inflatable bathtub.
✓ Use a baby-size bath sponge.
✓ Place a laundry basket in the bath.
✓ Use bath seats or bath rings with care.

Managing the Toys
✓ Circulate the toys.
✓ Double up on bath toys.
✓ Store toys in a laundry basket.
✓ Use mesh bags.

BEFORE STARTING

Giving your twins a bath does not have to be an anxiety-filled experience. Do whatever you can to make yourself less worried and more comfortable, including involving your spouse in the process.

Accept, but Don't Get Overwhelmed by, Your Anxiety

It's common to worry about how to bathe your baby. A wet baby is not only tiny, fragile, and slippery, but probably crying because he doesn't like the cold or the sensation of being wet. Meanwhile, you're also worried about the water temperature, the awkwardness of the tub or the sink, and your own utter lack of experience. The biggest concern generally is that your baby will slip out of your grasp in the water. With twins, you have twice the anxiety. These are normal feelings, and once you get some practice washing your babies, you'll become adept at giving baths. After the first month or so, you'll probably wonder why you got all worked up about it in the first place.

Limit Your Anxiety by Reducing the Number of Baths

Babies do not have to get a bath daily. If you're super stressed out, don't force yourself to give them a bath every single day. Give them a bath every other day, or every three or four days. If you feel your twins really do need a bath, then bathe the babies on different days—that way, you only have to worry about one baby at a time. The downside to that approach is that although you may have a lower level of anxiety about giving one baby a bath, you'll also have more anxious days than if you give both babies a bath on that same day and make other days entirely "bath free."

BATHING STRATEGIES

There's not one best way to bathe twins, but keep in mind that you're not necessarily limited to bathing them in your bathroom.

Bathe the Babies in the Kitchen Sink

Start by giving your twins baths in the kitchen sink. This allows you to stand rather than having to crouch and reach uncomfortably as you would while kneeling beside a standard bathtub. If you can make yourself more comfortable for at least the first few baths, you'll reduce your stress level (which you invariably communicate to your babies). Just how you can give your twins a bath in the sink depends on its width and depth, as well as how much counter space you have available. A small baby bathtub may fit in a particularly large sink; if you have a smaller sink, you may have to improvise. One good strategy is to buy a little folding mesh seat and place one baby on it in the sink while you wash her. Make sure you have a small container of warm water on hand, too, to hold washcloths.

Bathe the Babies in the Shower

If you have a shower that's separate from your tub, it may be easier for you to place a baby bathtub in the shower stall, fill it up, and bathe your babies while sitting or kneeling by the open shower door. This option works particularly well if you have a tub that is too deep for you to comfortably kneel beside to give the babies a bath.

Bathe the Babies in Other Rooms

You don't have to be resigned to using a small bathroom to give baths. If you have a baby bathtub, spread out into the house and move to the living room or kitchen. One baby can lie beside you or sit in a baby swing while you bathe the other. Just be sure to protect your floor or carpet by placing some towels or a rubber mat under the tub, and again, bring a container to hold your wet washcloths.

Involve Two Adults and Split the Responsibilities

It's easiest if two people can work together to give the babies a bath. You can set up an assembly line where one person washes both babies, while the other dries, diapers, and dresses them. Alternatively, you and your spouse can wash and dress one baby each. If you know your partner or spouse (or mom, sister, or friend) will help with bathing the twins, just make sure to invest in two baby bathtubs—it will save you time.

Bathe with the Babies

If there are two adults present, it may be easier for everyone involved if you bathe in the tub with your babies. One adult sits in the tub with Baby A while the other watches Baby B. After the bath, the adult in the tub hands off Baby A to the other adult to be dried and dressed, then proceeds to give Baby B a bath.

WHEN YOU HAVE AN OLDER CHILD

Your toddler or preschooler will want to be front and center when you give the babies a bath. An older child will want to feel involved, too.

Involve Your Older Child

If you have a toddler or preschooler, you'll find that he or she seems to be particularly underfoot when it's bath time for the twins. Give your older child a job, such as handing you towels or washing the twins' hair gently with a washcloth. Our daughter was only two and half when her brother and sister were born, and she was fascinated by the babies' bath time. I put her to work by having her wet a washcloth and wash the babies' hands and feet. After five or ten minutes, the novelty would be over and she'd wander off to her room or sit outside the bathroom and play quietly with a toy. School-age children can do more substantive tasks for toddler twins, like running the bathwater or shampooing their hair.

Bathe the Twins and an Older Child Together

Another way to keep everyone happy is to give your older a child a bath while you bathe the twins (no kidding, it can be done!). Fill the large bathtub to a fairly low level and place the baby bathtub inside. Your toddler or preschooler can splash in the big tub while you give the twins a bath in the baby tub. It helps if you put in bubbles or a special bath toy for your older child, so she is not constantly touching the babies.

Distract Your Older Child

Blowing bubbles is a great bathroom activity (there's less chance of creating a mess in the bathroom than anywhere else in the house). Washing pretend dishes in the sink or in a separate bowl of sudsy water is another game that may engage your older child. Bath time for the twins is also an opportunity to let your older child do something special, like watch a special video or page through a photo album.

WHEN YOU'RE ALONE

If you have to handle bath time by yourself, keeping both babies close by and safe is the central challenge. Use any means you can to keep both babies near you—a car seat, a bouncy seat, a Boppy pillow, or a swing all work well, as do Exersaucers for older babies.

Use Accessories

How do you safely give one baby a bath while watching the other, especially if your bathroom is far from the babies' cribs? Use items that will keep both babies close by. Depending on the size of your bathroom you can seat one baby in a bouncy seat, a car seat, or even a swing, while you give the other a bath. If these items won't fit in your bathroom, then put them right outside the bathroom door.

Use Hooded Towels

Hooded towels are great for keeping your babies warm. Avoid the typical thin hooded towels and invest in some pricier but considerably warmer ones. Pottery Barn Kids and Lillian Vernon have some good products.

Undress and Dress Your Babies in the Bathroom

I used to bring my babies into the bathroom in their bouncy seats. I'd also bring in their pajamas, diapers, and diaper cream. Instead of carrying them back to their room to get dressed (where they might catch a chill), I simply dressed them in their pajamas in the bathroom. I'd undress and bathe one baby, dress him in his pajamas, then undress and bathe his sister.

Warm Up the Water Between Babies

Unlike parents of singletons who only have to fill their baby tubs once, be sure to refill your bathtub before washing your second baby. If you can't or don't have the time to refill it entirely, at least add some hot water, so the twin who's getting bathed second has the benefit of some warm water, too.

Bring in Two Towels for Each Baby

If you can't get your baby dressed immediately after her bath, be sure to wrap her up in a couple of towels so that she stays warm while you bathe her twin. Simply spread one towel on whatever surface you plan to put your baby on after her bath, then sit her in it, wrap her, and cover her with a second towel.

Bring in Two Small Seats or Pillows

If you have space in your bathroom, bring in two items where you can set your babies down. You can never predict when you'll need to have both hands free. While one of your babies is sitting in his chair by the tub, you may have to suddenly rush and put your second, possibly naked, baby down in his crib, which may be far off in another room. It cuts down on stress if you are armed with two seats or pillows in the bathroom.

Bring a Bottle and Bottle Prop, Just in Case

Another tip for keeping the baby that's not being bathed at that particular moment quiet and content is to bring a bottle and a bottle prop with you into the bathroom.

Bathe Them Together When the Twins Can Sit Up

Once your babies can sit up, you can put them both in the tub at the same time. Just be sure to take your time getting the babies used to the big bathtub and keep the water level low, about two to three inches, so that even if they slide down or lie on their bellies they won't swallow water. And be sure to sit beside them the entire time.

MAKING BATH TIME MORE COMFORTABLE FOR YOU

There are some general strategies to make the process of bathing your babies easier and more comfortable for you.

Protect Your Knees

If you're bathing your twins in a bathtub, protect your knees and increase your comfort by folding and placing a towel under them. A bath rug helps, but adding a folded towel really makes that hard floor bearable for the twenty minutes or so the bath takes.

Store Towels and Washcloths Within Easy Reach

It's important not only to have extra towels and washcloths available when giving your twins a bath, but to make sure they're within easy reach of your outstretched hand. Remember that you'll be kneeling at the bath rather than standing up, so it's pointless to store towels or washcloths up high on shelves or towel racks that are mounted far up on a wall. Instead, keep essentials under the sink, or buy a small rack or container that you can reach into while still keeping a hand on your baby.

Install a Faucet Guard

Faucet or spout guards are soft, insulated covers that are easy to install. They come in especially handy with older twins who can sit up on their own or who can pull themselves up and may potentially hit their heads against the faucet during a bath. Faucet guards are also great if you have a sloped bathtub and your kids slide toward the front of the tub.

Keep Extra Towels Handy

Your twins don't have to be splash-happy toddlers for you to get soaked while giving them a bath. You will get wet regardless of their age, and it's likely that your bathroom will become a minor flood zone, too. Keep extra towels handy that you can use to drape over yourself or to wipe down the floor.

CHOOSING BATH AIDS

Inflatable bathtubs, laundry baskets, and bath mats are just some of the items you may find indispensable when bathing your twins.

Get a Rubber Mat

Make your bathtub a lot less slippery by getting a rubber mat or affixing some rubber decals in the tub. A mat is especially helpful once your babies can sit up and you try giving them a bath together.

Try an Inflatable Bathtub

Some parents of twins love inflatable bathtubs. Although we never used them, I can see the appeal. An inflatable bathtub placed inside the large bath helps secure your babies into a smaller space, plus it gives squirmy, wobbly toddlers a soft place to land if they should slip. You can even buy cute duck-shaped tubs, which are a big hit with younger children.

Use a Baby-Size Bath Sponge

If you don't want to buy a baby bathtub or want to make the baby tub more comfortable, get an inexpensive sponge at Babies "R" Us or another baby store. These baby-size sponges keep infants secure, even when placed inside a standard bathtub. They are also inexpensive, lightweight, and portable, so you can buy two or replace them when they get worn out. Plus, unlike a baby bathtub that can be bulky to handle when you're trying to clean it, all you have to do with the sponges is wring them out to dry.

Place a Laundry Basket in the Bath

A very inexpensive but effective way to keep both babies sitting securely together in the bath is to put them in a laundry basket. Many moms swear by this method, because both babies are together and can sit upright with just enough room to splash around. You can make the basket more secure by placing it on top of some rubber decals or a rubber mat in the tub. One thing to look out for is that some active babies may be able to tip the basket over.

Use Bath Seats or Bath Rings with Care

Bath seats, sometimes called bath rings, are hugely popular with mothers of twins because they let both babies sit upright so that one person can wash them. These molded plastic seats have a plastic ring that supports the baby at the waist and uses suction cups to adhere to the bathtub. Many moms swear there's no way in the world they'll give their twins a bath alone without this device. Popular brands include the Safety 1st Tubside Bath Seat, which has an elbow cushion for the parent, and The First Years Tub-to-Seat Bath Complete, which clamps to the side of the tub for safety. But even though these seats are a favorite with parents of twins, there are some safety concerns. For example, some parents say that some models have problems suctioning properly, so the seat could slide or tip over. And older babies (around eight months or so) may want to crawl out of the seats, which is also dangerous. The biggest concern may be that parents will overrely on the seats and leave their babies unsupervised in the bathtub, which is unsafe and is *not* recommended.

MANAGING THE TOYS

At some point, bath toys will take over your bathroom. There are ways to restrain the chaos, though.

Circulate the Toys

There are only so many toys you can fit in your house, not to mention in a small bathroom. Keep the majority under wraps and let your twins play with a select few toys. After a few days or a week, put those toys away and bring out some new ones. What's old becomes new again after your kids haven't seen them for a while.

Double Up on Bath Toys

Unlike regular toys, bath toys seem to be especially coveted, perhaps because the bathtub is small and each twin can always see what the other is playing with and reach over to grab it. Save yourself a lot of yelling and screeching and just buy two of everything, or buy toys that come in multiples, such as foam cutouts. Inflatable balls, bubble makers (the kind that come with a wand), and plastic containers or plastic tea sets are excellent bath toys.

Store Toys in a Laundry Basket

The lowly laundry basket does double-duty in the bathroom. As mentioned earlier in this chapter, you can put both your twins inside to keep them secure while bathing them. Once they've outgrown that, you can use the basket to store all of the dripping-wet bath toys. Laundry baskets work particularly well for twins and their parents, because you're likely to have far more toys than parents of singletons and the baskets are inexpensive, dry easily, and require no extra storage space (they sit right in the tub to dry).

Use Mesh Bags

Keep a small selection of your babies' favorite bath toys in mesh bags that use suction cups to adhere to the bathroom walls. Although they are not really practical for storing many toys, since they can slowly slide down the wall or peel away entirely if they're too full, they are great for storing and keeping a small number of toys within ready reach.

PART THREE

LEAVING THE HOUSE

11

Making Errands Possible

Try going to the grocery store—or doing any errand, for that matter—while you're alone with the babies. That pretty much sums up the challenges of parenting twins: There are two of them and only one of you. It seems impossible to manage the kids, the gear, the headaches, and tears (yours and theirs) and still get out of the house. But as any parent of twins knows, there will be times when you absolutely, positively need to run out to buy something (diapers, formula, a winning lottery ticket so you can afford that nanny) while you're minding the babies. And there'll also be times that you'll go stir-crazy unless you can get out and about among people, babies or not.

There are basically two strategies for shopping with twins, or with twins and another child: You have to learn to become a pack mule, carrying the extra baby, diapers, and food somewhere on your body, or you can enlist a spouse, parent, child, or stranger to help you. Regardless of which of the two strategies you rely on, it's also important that you consider your destination to help ensure (if possible) that aisles and carts are wide enough for you and your clan and that you can find some privacy if necessary.

The good news is that it *is* possible to get out of the house. Just invest in an excellent stroller, prepare the gear and yourself ahead of time, and have fun, knowing that life gets easier as you become more proficient at everything you thought was impossible. Here goes.

Strategies for Shopping with Twins
✓ Shop with two carts.
✓ Connect the carts.

✓ Patronize stores with drive-throughs.
✓ Have groceries delivered.
✓ Get an assistant.
✓ Shop at stores with double shopping carts.
✓ Put a baby in a Boppy.
✓ Shop with your stroller.
✓ Use a backpack or front pack.
✓ Shop at family-friendly stores.
✓ Put your baby in a sling (or two).
✓ Play tag team.

Strategies for Shopping with Three or More Children

✓ Put three in a cart.
✓ Maneuver two in a cart, plus one.
✓ Use a backpack carrier.
✓ Get a wrist strap.
✓ Use a safety harness.
✓ Bring toys to distract your older child.

Preparing the Gear and Yourself

✓ Pack food separately.
✓ Make "quick change" bags.
✓ Carry a couple of receiving blankets.
✓ Take medicine.
✓ Grab a banana.
✓ Write lists and focus on what you need.
✓ Wear clothes with pockets.
✓ Prepare your car.
✓ Keep at least one front pack or backpack in the car.
✓ Use two diaper bags.

STRATEGIES FOR SHOPPING WITH TWINS

There's no reason you can't go shopping if you have twins. Just consider it an exercise in creativity (and be prepared for the possibility that you may get some stares).

Shop with Two Carts

Shopping with two carts works—just barely—and is bound to draw a lot of attention to you and your babies (as if you didn't get enough already!). But sometimes you have no other choice. Basically, you push the babies and your baby paraphernalia in one cart and pull a second cart for holding your groceries or other items. It's unwieldy and takes some extra time, but you can get everything you need in one trip. Just be careful when turning corners.

Connect the Carts

Buy a six-inch bungee cord (or shorter, if available) at your local hardware store and carry it in your car or purse. You can use the cord to attach two separate carts, which means you only have to pull one cart instead of pushing and pulling two.

Patronize Stores with Drive-Throughs

Sometimes, as a new parent, errands are more about simply getting out of the house than getting things done. Especially in winter, I found there were times when it was enough to just leave my house and go somewhere with a purpose. I didn't need to shop; I just needed to do something that wasn't baby-related (even if I did have to take the babies with me). I found I could run all sorts of errands at places with drive-throughs: from getting food to picking up medicine, magazines, or photos; cashing or depositing checks; or even renting movies. In some cases I called ahead, provided stores with my debit or credit card information, and had one of their employees run things out to my car. Or, in the case of the pharmacy, I would call ahead to get nonpharmacy items at the drive-through window. The local McDonald's or KFC restaurant, my bank, my corner pharmacy, even my dry cleaner became destinations of choice—all because I could drive there, get something accomplished, and not have to deal with moving my kids in and out of car seats and into strollers. That one or two hours out of the house was enough to put me back in good spirits, and as a bonus, I got things done!

Have Groceries Delivered

Many grocery stores offer home delivery. Check their policy before you phone in your order so you know what their process is. In some areas of the country there are online services, such as Peapod, that allow you to order groceries online and have them delivered to your door. These services are well worth the money for parents who need to shop but can't do so alone or just don't have the time while caring for two babies. Having groceries delivered is one of the best gifts for parents of newborn twins—it's one less thing for sleep-deprived moms and dads to worry about.

Get an Assistant

When you are at your local store, ask if someone can help you push your cart. Grocery baggers usually provide assistance out to your car and they may be able to help you while you're inside as well. Ask the customer service or store manager, or phone ahead if you know you'll be needing help.

Shop at Stores with Double Shopping Carts

Shopping at stores with double shopping carts works when your babies are very small and happily tucked into their infant carriers, as well as when they're a few months old and able to sit on their own in the front of the shopping cart. Costco, Meijer, Sam's Club, and other stores have extralarge shopping carts that let you sit both babies up front. Suzanna, my coworker, made this suggestion to me when I was pregnant, and I heeded her advice. For months after my twins were born I loved shopping at my local Costco mainly because I only had to push one cart. In addition, these chains are usually one-stop stores that carry groceries and prescription drugs; offer photo-developing services; and sell household items, clothes, and most important, diapers, formula, and wipes.

Put a Baby in a Boppy

Keep a Boppy pillow and extra blankets in your car. At stores where you can only fit one baby's car seat in the shopping cart, take your second baby and put him in a Boppy in the large basket. A friend of mine would bring the cart up to her car in the parking lot, then put one baby in her car seat in the front and the other on a blanket in the Boppy in the basket. She liked this strategy because her baby girls both loved looking around at all the different sights, and she didn't feel like a pack mule with everything on her back.

Shop with Your Stroller

This advice may be obvious, but it bears reminding that shopping with your stroller has to be worth it in terms of the time it takes you to set up your stroller and pack everyone and everything into it. You also have to be able to navigate your stroller wherever you plan to shop. Stroller shopping is a great solution when you're in a store or a mall with lots of wide spaces, or if you are out window-shopping or simply need to pick up a few things. Once the babies are strapped in you're good to go. The downside is that you can only buy what you can put in or on your stroller, or on your back in a backpack.

Use a Backpack or Front Pack

Backpacks and front packs are among the many things that are indispensable to mothers of twins. A front pack lets you carry one baby on your body so you can use your arms to carry the second baby in a car seat or simply hold on to the multiple bags and items (like a purse) you're inevitably going to be carrying. Similarly, backpacks let you carry tons of gear but leave your hands free to manage your babies. Specialized backpacks can also be used to carry an older baby.

Buy a backpack big enough to hold food, clothes, or any of the miscellaneous stuff you'll discover you need (usually at the precise moment you're handling the two babies by yourself) and keep it in your car. Then, with your babies in a shopping cart or in a stroller, you can put your purchases in a pack you can wear on your back or hang off your cart or stroller. One mom, whose twins are now five, used to keep three different backpacks in her car when her boys were younger. One backpack was just for food (so she didn't mind it getting banged up or spilled on), one was a smaller backpack for mini-shopping trips, and one was a large, wide pack she could fit a winter jacket into. Or, in a modified version of the Boppy trick, have one baby ride in a car seat at the front of the shopping cart while you carry the second baby in a front pack. However, this strategy pretty much depends on how much your babies like being carried.

Shop at Family-Friendly Stores

You'll find that it makes your life easier when you shop at family-friendly stores, especially those with nursing rooms or lounge areas. Ikea, Babies "R" Us, and department stores have better-than-average facilities for moms (and dads) and babies, including nursing rooms, ladies' lounges, and even dressing rooms. For longer shopping trips, it's critical to find facilities with a sofa or large chair, so you can spread out to feed and change the babies, and that has enough room to accommodate your enormous stroller. Go to the ladies' or children's areas in department stores. The workers there tend to be more understanding and accommodating since they see moms with kids all the time.

Put Your Baby in a Sling (or Two)

Unlike a front pack, a sling lets you adjust your baby so you can carry him over your hip; more important, you can crisscross two slings and carry both babies simultaneously, leaving your hands free to push a cart. You need to practice maneuvering with this getup at home before attempting to take the babies out, however. Some moms are uncomfortable carrying both babies in slings because it makes them feel like the babies are too precariously balanced. (This was my experience, I have to admit.) On the other hand, some moms do it all the time. One mom of twins I know had both her babies in slings at a party!

Play Tag Team

If you're lucky enough to have someone help you, use the tag team approach for shorter shopping trips. As long as there are two adults (or even one adult and a teenager), one person can sit in the car babysitting while the other shops. Make sure to organize the trips so that the stores appeal to both of you and your trips inside don't take too long. There's nothing worse than having to listen to your husband complain that you took forever in Target while he was stuck in the car, or about having to stop at both Target *and* Babies "R" Us. Throw a little Home Depot in the mix and you sit in the car while he goes in the store.

STRATEGIES FOR SHOPPING WITH THREE OR MORE CHILDREN

You are in for some strategizing here, and there are fewer options, but shopping with twins and another child (or children) can be done. You'll just need to rely on bigger carts, carrying aids, or harnesses, and loads of patience.

Put Three in a Cart
Three in a cart is possible with double or extra-wide carts, or sometimes with novelty carts, such as the truck- and police car–themed carts you sometimes see in grocery stores.

Maneuver Two in a Cart, Plus One
If the store has regular-size shopping carts, the older child sits in the front of the cart, one newborn sits in a car seat in the large basket, and the second baby is in a front pack or sling that you carry on your body. Just know that you'll have limited space for your groceries or other "stuff."

Use a Backpack Carrier
If you have a toddler, carry her in a toddler-appropriate backpack carrier. These backpacks are also great if you plan to travel or go camping. They range in price from about $40 to more than $100 but often can support children up to forty-five pounds.

Get a Wrist Strap
If you have a preschooler as well as twins, a wrist strap can be a lifesaver. Your older child can walk along with you while you put both babies in a cart. That way, you don't have to worry about your preschooler wandering off. One thing to note: You may get some stares or remarks about being a cruel parent. Ignore them. When you have no way to carry three (or four) children but still need to eat, shop, and get other things done, you have to rely on help. Or, if people comment and it really bugs you, ask them to help. You'll

either get some desperately needed assistance or the satisfaction of having the last word.

Use a Safety Harness
Safety harnesses go around the child's torso and can generate even more comments than a wrist strap, but they really keep your older child safe.

Bring Toys to Distract Your Older Child
Either bring along your children's favorites, or set aside some special toys that you only allow on shopping trips to keep their full attention and discourage whining and tantrums.

PREPARING THE GEAR AND YOURSELF

Getting your gear, yourself, and your car ready ahead of time is one of the biggest keys to success. You'll have to pack diapers, blankets, bottles, and lotions for the babies. But be especially kind to yourself and bring drinks and food, too.

Pack Food Separately
Yes, you will need that enormous diaper bag on your shopping trip, but most often you need quick access to a couple of bottles (if you're bottle-feeding), milk or juice, or some kid snacks. Insulated lunch bags work great. They're small, inexpensive, and can sit in the front part of the cart in plain view. Throw in an icepack, a couple of bottles, and you're set.

Make "Quick Change" Bags
Use plastic freezer bags to pack one diaper, a few wipes, and, if you want, some travel packs of diaper cream. Prepare a couple of these packs for each baby and put them in your diaper bag. That way, when you reach into the bag you are not rooting around searching for that elusive diaper or container of wipes while your twins cry ever more loudly. Instead, you have everything you need in a single-use bag. When you're done, you can throw the freezer bag away. (On the other hand, if you're really interested in recycling, you can take that single-use bag, clean it, and repurpose it for another time.)

Carry a Couple of Receiving Blankets
Bring a couple of receiving blankets with you at all times. They make great bottle props, do double-duty as changing mats, and keep your babies warm.

Take Medicine

Carry Advil or Tylenol and a bottle of water in the car for your whopping headache. This tip comes care of my husband, who was the king of stress when the babies were small. Trust me, shopping with twins (or more children) *will* be stressful. We'd pack up all three kids, get bundled up (it was winter), and then after ten minutes of being at the store, he'd get crabby and rush me to finish up because he had a headache. Do yourself a favor and keep something for your (or your husband's) inevitable headache with you at all times.

Grab a Banana

Having a banana or some trail mix with you can be another lifesaver. This tip isn't meant to prevent you from overbuying at the grocery store, but it is a way to stave off headaches due to energy crashes. So many parents of twins tell me that they just don't have the time—or, ironically, the energy—to eat. Then they decide to leave the house and wrangle two wailing babies into the car. And as soon as they get to their destination, they realize they're hungry and don't have the energy to do anything else except go home. Be kind to yourself and carry some snacks in your purse or diaper bag.

Write Lists and Focus on What You Need

Once again, it may seem like an obvious point, but you will get baby brain with twins. You will go to a store and not remember what you came for, or you'll get there and feel rushed as the babies start to cry. The key is to be organized and give yourself as much help as possible. Write a shopping or to-do list before you leave the house.

Wear Clothes with Pockets

Don't underestimate the sheer amount of stuff you'll have practically slipping through your fingers. Diaper backpacks are great, but you still need somewhere to hold your car keys, your wallet, and one or two pacifiers. Make it simple and wear clothes with pockets.

Prepare Your Car

Preparing your car means having a second set of anything you might conceivably use when going out on errands. A coworker of mine kept an extra diaper bag in his car, prepacked with nonperishables for the occasional impromptu trip. "It just saved my sanity knowing I didn't have to run around and collect everything in the world before we could leave the house. We would just pack up some food and go," he told me. Think about packing receiving blankets, diapers, wipes (or some "quick change" bags), extra pacifiers, hand disinfectant, rattles, trail mix, and anything else you might need, like a pen or a notepad. Make sure to have some pain relievers and a small bottle of water while you're at it.

Keep at Least One Front Pack or Backpack in the Car

More often than not, you will be running out the door and simply forget that one crucial thing you need to help you carry a baby—a front pack or backpack. If it's already in your car, it's one less thing to worry about.

Use Two Diaper Bags

Some parents of twins prepare a diaper bag or backpack for each baby, doubling up on everything, including insulated bags for food. This two-bag system is great when you and your spouse go out together but end up going your separate ways in the store.

12

Preparing, Packing, and Bundling Your Twins for a Car Ride

Taking your twins on a car ride has its own challenges. Even a short ride demands a lot of preparation and packing, plus the challenge of getting the babies ready to go before they have a meltdown. If you're managing the babies on your own, it's not unusual for the preparation to far exceed the time you're out, because then you have to figure out a way to singlehandedly get all of your gear and your twins out to the car safely and quickly. Longer car trips also challenge your abilities to distract your twins. A successful car trip depends on the sequence of how you do things, plus the gear you take. Here are some suggestions.

Getting Your Babies in the Car
✓ Stage everything you'll need first.
✓ Get yourself ready, then get the twins ready.
✓ If there are two of you, pack the car first.
✓ If you're alone, restrain the babies in their infant car seat carriers first.
✓ Move everything in stages if you live on a high floor.
✓ Use a wheeled car seat carrier to transport things.
✓ Plan your trips around your twins' nap time.

Arranging the Seats
✓ Maximize seating space.
✓ Beware of tricky seat-belt placement.

Taking Long Trips with Twins
✓ Drive at night.
✓ Dress your children for sleep.

✓ Leave in the wee hours if you don't like to drive at night.
✓ Make your first leg the longest.
✓ Adopt electronic tolling.
✓ Bring earplugs.
✓ Block the light.
✓ Turn the car seats forward.
✓ Use a dual DVD player.
✓ Try switching car seats after breaks.
✓ Stretch your legs.
✓ Eat outside whenever possible.
✓ Take side trips if possible.

What to Bring
✓ Stock the essentials.
✓ Keep a cooler within easy reach.
✓ Bring the babies' blankets and pillows in the car.
✓ Bring sweaters or jackets.
✓ Invest in toy organizers for the car.
✓ Bring a couple of extra changes of clothes.
✓ Use headphones.

Good Distractions
✓ Install child-safe mirrors.
✓ Double up on popular toys.
✓ Avoid toys that can become projectiles.
✓ Play music.
✓ Bring books.
✓ Bring out new toys.
✓ Bring favorite toys.
✓ Create "goody bags."
✓ Hand out toys one at a time.
✓ Bring forbidden foods.
✓ Keep a stash of "last resort" treats.

GETTING YOUR BABIES IN THE CAR

Getting your babies in the car requires planning. Be prepared to work ahead, then to run like the wind, especially if 1) you don't have a garage and need to park on the street; 2) you're trying to pack everything by yourself, including the babies; or 3) you live on a high floor and have to go up and down steps or elevators.

Stage Everything You'll Need First

Prepare snacks and bottles, then pack diapers, wipes, and anything else you might need first and leave it by the door closest to your car. You'll avoid forgetting essentials if you gather them well before you have to leave. You'll also know how much space you'll need to store all of the stuff you're taking. Even a short errand may require packing a lot of stuff and reorganizing your car. We found that it took about twenty to thirty minutes to prepare and pack formula, then pack the diaper bag, plus an additional fifteen to twenty minutes just to dress ourselves and load the car. The babies added another fifteen minutes. Basically, we could not get out of the house unless we began getting ready forty-five minutes to an hour in advance.

Get Yourself Ready, Then Get the Twins Ready

The trick with babies (especially twins) and car rides is that the babies need to be handled last, or else they'll get too cranky, hungry, or wet by the time you're set to go. Take the time to get yourself ready first, so that you're calm and collected, then change and dress the twins. The only exception is if you need to wear winter coats, in which case dress the babies in their jackets or coats first before putting on yours. There's nothing worse in the winter than trying to wedge two babies into small car seats while you're wearing your bulky winter coat.

If There Are Two of You, Pack the Car First

While one person dresses and gets the babies ready for the trip, the other person should be packing the car. Two people doing the work gives you a big advantage in terms of getting everyone and everything ready, since you don't have to worry about leaving the babies alone while you go out and get the car packed.

If You're Alone, Restrain the Babies in Their Infant Car Seat Carriers First

As a parent of twins, you're nearly always forced to make a choice between doing things and watching the babies. You can carry stuff out to the car or you can carry both babies, but you can't do both unless you have help. If you're by yourself, prepare and stage everything first, then restrain the babies before carrying your things out to the car. It's easier and safer if the babies go in last. They'll be quite safe sitting secured in their car seats inside your house.

Move Everything in Stages If You Live on a High Floor

One mom I interviewed for this book lived in a third-floor apartment, which made carting the babies and their stuff nearly impossible. Basically, she moved everything, including her twins, into her car in stages. She prepared everything beforehand, then put the babies in their car seats and fed them by propping up two bottles. During the time they ate, she ran downstairs and hurried and packed her car, then returned to her apartment for the twins, carrying them both at the same time in their carriers. On the return trip home, she first carried the babies upstairs and inside her apartment, then went back to the car for her stuff. When it was impossible to either leave things in her car or to leave her babies unattended in her apartment, she moved everyone and everything over small distances. First, she brought her things to the door to her building, then returned to her car for the babies. Next, she took her twins inside to the second landing, then went back and moved her things. The key was that she kept both the babies and her other belongings in view the entire time.

Use a Wheeled Car Seat Carrier to Transport Things

The wheeled bags designed to protect your car seat in the airport (see Chapter 13 for some recommendations) can be put to use in your everyday life. Instead of using them to store your bulky car seat, keep one in the back of your car for those occasions when you have a lot of stuff but still have to carry your babies. The bags can accommodate bulky items, but take care that you don't overload them so that they're super heavy, because you may not be able to lift them up curbs or stairs. Look for a bag that has a reinforced or hard bottom, which will give the bag some shape (and keep your things from getting too crushed). And definitely read product reviews from users on the Internet, because some brands look great but seem to rip quickly or are hard to navigate. Bags by J. L. Childress Co., Inc. and by Go-Go Babyz are pretty sturdy, although you'll need a separate wheel apparatus (the gogo Kidz Travelmate) if you choose the latter brand.

Plan Your Trips Around Your Twins' Nap Time

You'll soon discover whether your twins travel better before or after they take a nap. Some parents opt to wait until after the babies have eaten and are changed before going out, knowing that they'll fall asleep in the car. Others prefer the reverse. They wait to go anywhere until their babies have woken up, so the babies can be calm and alert instead of fussing during the drive. Pay attention on your first couple of errands and take your cues from the babies.

ARRANGING THE SEATS

Space is tight with two or three car seats. Adjust the car seat arrangements and pay close attention to safe car seat installation.

Maximize Seating Space

Count yourself lucky if you have a van. For a family with twins a van is a luxury, and for a family with twins plus other children, it is a virtual necessity. If you have a sedan or station wagon, as we do, having three car seats in the backseat is a very, very tight fit. You'll get the most room if you have a convertible car seat in the center of the back row, with an infant-carrier car seat on each side. Once your twins move into convertible seats, your older child may have to move to a booster seat (either one that's built into the car or one that you purchase at the store). If you believe that arrangement will be impossible, given your children's ages, then look for the narrowest convertible seats you can find. And measure your car's back row and measure the car seats, too, before buying them.

Beware of Tricky Seat-Belt Placement

If you install your twins' car seats side-by-side in the back row of your car and you're using seat belts to secure them, watch that during installation you don't inadvertently unlock one of the seat belts. The problem is that the lock for the middle seat belt is located beside one of locks for the side seat belts, so it's very easy to inadvertently press one of the buttons and unlock the middle seat belt while installing a car seat next to it. You could end up driving only to discover midway through your trip that one of the car seats is not actually secured (as happened to us once).

TAKING LONG TRIPS WITH TWINS

Car trips with twins are not that much different from car trips with other children, except that you'll generally have only one set of issues to deal with since your kids are the same age. That said, if you're traveling with twins, or with twins and another child, you want to work with them, not against them, on a long trip.

Drive at Night

Maximize peaceful and uninterrupted driving time by traveling at night. Pack your car so that your babies go in last. Then leave shortly before the babies' late-afternoon nap or at bedtime (an hour before works pretty well). The babies will probably be alert for a while, then will drift off to sleep and will probably sleep uninterrupted until morning, which will leave you with long stretches of time to focus on driving. When our twins were two and our oldest was four, we drove nearly a thousand miles, from Chicago to Connecticut, or about eighteen hours each way. Driving at night was certainly difficult—we took turns sleeping and slept fewer hours than we normally would—but it was worth it in terms of the peace and quiet and the time we saved by having to make fewer stops while on the road.

Dress Your Children for Sleep

To encourage our children to fall asleep before our nighttime drive, we prepared a mini-nighttime routine for them in the late afternoon. We had an early dinner, then gave all the kids a bath and put on their pajamas. We were on the road at 6:30 p.m., about forty-five minutes before our twins usually fell asleep. Ironically, our four-year-old fell asleep first, about an hour into our trip, while our twins stayed awake—but quiet—much longer.

Leave in the Wee Hours If You Don't Like to Drive at Night

If you really don't want to drive at night, leave very early in the morning, between 2:00 and 4:00 a.m. Make sure your car is completely packed before your trip and stocked with drinks, snacks, and toys, all within easy reach. Then take your sleeping twins and put them in their car seats. It helps tremendously if both parents carry the twins out to the car, to limit the time they will be disrupted. It's very likely your twins will simply fall back asleep until their regular wake-up time.

Make Your First Leg the Longest

Somehow the novelty of the car trip extends only to the first or possibly the second rest stop, then it becomes a terrible confinement. If you begin driving at night, you can make that first leg of your journey go as long as twelve hours, barring tollbooth stops, fill-ups, and bathroom runs for the adults. In the morning, however, you will probably find that the twins want to get out and don't want to come back in.

Adopt Electronic Tolling

Many states now use electronic toll-collection systems on their highways. If you live in one of these states, be sure to take advantage of this option, because it will allow you to speed through the tollbooth stops instead of waiting in long cash-payment lines.

Bring Earplugs

On long car trips, one adult is generally trying to rest while the other drives. Bring earplugs to drown out the ruckus your twins will undoubtedly make and to ensure that you get some sleep. Earplugs come in particularly handy at night, or when your preschoolers launch into their tenth rendition of "Row, Row, Row Your Boat."

Block the Light

One of the more irritating things we experienced when driving at night was that the kids were sound asleep until we stopped at a tollbooth. Stopping in the bright lights even for forty-five seconds got them stirring and, in a couple of cases, crying. Additionally, most of the nighttime traffic consisted of tractor-trailer trucks, whose lights inevitably shone brightly into our car, especially as we slowed down to pay tolls. Use sunshades on the windows next to the twins to help block out the light—but be sure to install and test them out before your big trip. Some parents think sunshades don't stay up well or actually block out too much light. In lieu of sunshades, you may want to drape a blanket loosely over the back of your babies' car seats, extending the edge of the blanket just over their eyes. Or, for a pricier and far more permanent option, consider getting your windows professionally tinted.

Turn the Car Seats Forward

Your twins may ride in car seats that face backward. But once they are old enough and big enough (at least one year and twenty pounds), use the long car trip as an occasion to turn their seats forward. The new view should be interesting enough to keep them occupied for a long portion of your trip.

Use a Dual DVD Player

Even if you're not a great believer in video games and entertainment for your babies, consider bringing along a DVD player. Portable DVD players are extremely effective for distracting your children and keeping them quiet on long car trips. These players, available from several manufacturers, install on the back of the front passenger seat headrest. Older kids may be able to use headphones, and for younger children, you can set the DVDs to play on a continuous loop so that you don't have to constantly stop or turn around awkwardly to change DVDs.

Try Switching Car Seats After Breaks

Sometimes twins may like the novelty of sitting in a different seat during the trip. Be aware, however, that other babies can get very attached to their own car seats and may refuse to move. Generally it's an all-or-nothing proposition.

Stretch Your Legs

Make frequent rest stops during the day. Stop for about ten minutes every hour, or for twenty minutes every two hours. Even if your twins are infants, make sure you stop and take them out of their car seats every couple of hours so that they can stretch and relax. Older children will want to run around, so seek out larger rest stops where there's some wide-open space or even a playground.

Eat Outside Whenever Possible

Take advantage of nice weather and do double-duty by choosing a rest stop where you can eat outside and where the kids can expend some energy. Toddlers and older children will really appreciate being "let loose." If your twins love trucks, they'll be happy to stay at a rest stop for far longer than you want to.

Take Side Trips If Possible

Depending on the length of your trip and how long you want to spend traveling, you can build in some quick side trips. Get off the highway and head into some of the towns or cities along the way, then head for some kid-friendly activities—a museum, zoo, or aquarium, or an offbeat roadside attraction. Even just a walk in a park or some time at a playground may do the trick.

WHAT TO BRING

You'll have to bring a large and varied number of essentials on longer car rides—everything from a cooler stocked with food and drinks to cleaning supplies, toys, and clothes.

Stock the Essentials

For a long car trip, you'll need to have not only snacks and drinks, but also items to clean up your car. Bring plenty of juice and water and extra cups with lids. Include protein-laden snacks, like cheese sticks or a container of cut-up hot dog. Avoid yogurt or cottage cheese or anything that needs to be eaten with a spoon, unless you plan on eating them when stopped. Also bring some quick-change diaper bags stocked with a diaper, wipes, and lotion, and keep them in easy reach (store one in the glove compartment as an emergency backup when you absolutely can't find diapers anywhere else). In terms of cleaning supplies, bring one full pack of wipes and a roll of paper towels to mop up spills. For really long trips, think about bringing a bottle of window cleaner as well, for cleaning off fingerprints, and some carpet cleaner or air freshener (in case your children get carsick or cause major spills). In addition, bring your kids' sunglasses or hats to help them manage daytime glare, and a portable potty and some toilet paper for kids who are newly potty-trained.

Keep a Cooler Within Easy Reach
Keep all foods that need to be refrigerated close by, and save space by bringing big containers of drinks and pouring individual servings into Sippy Cups as the kids ask for drinks. For infant twins, pack bottles for each baby in a separate container so that you can quickly reach in and get them, and also know how much each baby has consumed. In addition, bring a bottle of water (it doesn't have to be refrigerated) so that you can periodically rinse out bottles.

Bring the Babies' Blankets and Pillows in the Car
Encourage sleeping by bringing a favorite blanket and pillow for each child in the car. If your children use pacifiers or stuffed animals in bed, bring those as well so that they're surrounded by all of their favorite and familiar things for the long ride.

Bring Sweaters or Jackets
Even if your trip takes place in the summer, keep jackets and sweaters in the car for everyone. Make them easily accessible because those middle-of-the-night rest stops that require you to step outside can be chilly and because blankets can fall off and become impossible to find in the dark. Think of these items of clothing as secondary insurance against the cold.

Invest in Toy Organizers for the Car
Older children who can reach forward will appreciate having organizers to stash their toys, and you'll like having a place they can put their used cups or tissues, too.

Bring a Couple of Extra Changes of Clothes
A change of clothes is a good idea, not just for the twins, but for you, too, in case you get spilled on or the weather changes dramatically during your trip.

Use Headphones
For nighttime travel or when your twins are sleeping, use headphones to listen to music or books, but if you're the driver, make sure what you're listening to isn't loud enough to block out noise that can alert you to trouble or danger (car brakes squealing or a siren, for example).

GOOD DISTRACTIONS

Infants will be quite happy on longer trips as long as they have some toys to touch and mouth and if you schedule frequent stops to give them a chance to stretch out. But older children, from toddlers on up, will definitely need distractions.

Install Child-Safe Mirrors
Since babies love looking at faces, put a couple of child-safe mirrors on the windows to entertain your littlest ones.

Double Up on Popular Toys
Even young children will tug and pull the popular toys out of their sibling's hands. Avoid crying and fights by doubling up on toys you know they both (or all) want. For us, the popular toys were maracas and coloring books, desired by the twins and their older sister.

Avoid Toys That Can Become Projectiles
Some toys are just not safe to bring in the car. They include anything heavy, or with sharp edges, or items that can be thrown, like blocks or die-cast cars.

Play Music
Bring CDs of your kids' favorite music or children's books on tape. Bring musical toys, like a tambourine, some maracas, or even some plain old rattles, so they can play along with the music, if you don't mind the noise.

Bring Books
Older children will appreciate having some books to read or page through. Choose board books for smaller twins.

Bring Out New Toys
A new toy, as long as it's easy to handle, will keep your little ones occupied for quite a while. The following are great toys to take on trips:

* Coloring books and crayons.
* Paper and washable markers.
* Markers that write only on specially made paper, like Crayola's Color Wonder products.
* Magna Doodle markers, which use a special water-filled pen to draw on a small canvas drawing surface.
* Light-up or glow-in-the-dark toys.
* Magnetic puzzles or pictures that attach to a flat surface. You can make your own version by using a metal cookie tray and some magnetic alphabet letters—just be sure to test your cookie sheet first, to make sure the pieces adhere to it. Magnetic toys are most appropriate for

older children (smaller children may put the pieces in their mouths, which can be dangerous).

Bring Favorite Toys

Don't leave on your trip without bringing at least one favorite toy for each of your children. You can also make these favorites "new" again by wrapping them as gifts.

Create "Goody Bags"

Goody bags aren't just fun at parties. Fill a few goody bags with multiple small toys that kids can enjoy unwrapping. Hand them out periodically throughout the trip.

Hand Out Toys One at a Time

The minimal space inside a car or van means you will have a limited supply of toys for your trip. If you start out by giving the twins all or most of their toys at the start, they'll get bored a lot more quickly than if you extend the novelty.

Bring Forbidden Foods

Another good trick is to let your kids eat those foods that are generally off-limits in your house. In our case, we don't eat chips, pretzels, or doughnuts at home. But those foods played a prominent part in our car ride. We knew the kids liked these foods, so we let them indulge. Chips and pretzels are good because even small children can hold them in their hands, plus you can extend the treat by handing out only small portions at a time (for example, every few miles). This can keep your children occupied for at least half an hour.

Keep a Stash of "Last Resort" Treats

When we traveled, we brought along a huge bag of lollipops. They were our absolutely "last resort" treats, handed out when the crying got out of hand. We kept them well hidden so the kids weren't constantly looking at them and asking for them.

13

Traveling by Plane

If you plan to travel by plane with your twins, salute yourself for bravery. Today's environment of near-constant travel delays, increased security, and reduced amenities for coach passengers means that air travel is frustrating enough for adults. Add two small children (or more) into the mix and you are setting yourself up for a challenge. However, that challenge is certainly manageable with patience, planning, and a degree of ingenuity. Your travel plans will go a lot more smoothly if you know what to expect during your trip, including any airline-specific rules; plan for the unexpected to happen; have the right equipment and supplies; and rely on your sense of humor. Here are some suggestions.

Before You Fly
✓ Do your research.
✓ Decide how many people are flying.
✓ Buy tickets for everyone on international flights.
✓ See what your airline offers and request it.
✓ Call the airline to check if your car seat will fit.
✓ Arrange for car seats at your destination.
✓ Plan for your arrival.
✓ Go by van.
✓ Take advantage of the extra carry-on baggage allowance.
✓ Pack strategically.

At the Airport
✓ Bring birth certificates and other emergency information.
✓ Use separate umbrella strollers.

✓ Use a backpack.

✓ Allow extra time to go through airport security.

✓ Dress your babies with airport security in mind.

✓ Don't count on preboarding.

✓ Engage the gate staff.

✓ Gate-check your strollers.

On the Flight

✓ Make friends with the flight attendants.

✓ Bring car seats just in case.

✓ Pack multiple "quick meal" bags.

✓ Bring a cover-up.

✓ Pack multiple "quick change" bags.

✓ Pack extra earplugs.

✓ Bring pacifiers or bottles.

✓ Pack snacks.

✓ Bring something to cuddle.

✓ Bring toys and surprises.

✓ Tether the toys.

✓ Seat your twins strategically.

✓ Bring a towel and change of clothing for each child.

When Traveling with Car Seats

✓ Avoid booking seats in the bulkhead or the back row.

✓ Choose the window and middle seats.

✓ Let one person install the car seats first.

✓ Install seats based on your child's age and weight.

✓ Book seats in rows one behind the other.

✓ Avoid other restraint devices.

Great Travel Gear

✓ Buy a Wheelie Car Seat Travel Bag by The Right Start.

✓ Buy a gogo Kidz Travelmate.

✓ Use stroller connectors.

✓ Have crib toys with Velcro.

✓ Bring along travel-size packets of pain relievers.

BEFORE YOU FLY

Successful air travel starts well before you board the plane. When flying with twins, plan for safety and comfort.

Do Your Research

Children are subject to all sorts of airline restrictions, including where they can or cannot sit, whether you'll have to pay for their tickets, and what you can bring on the plane. This means that you must invest some time in researching your flight options, not only in terms of ticket cost, but what you need to buy, bring, or rent for your trip. We found that two months is about just enough time to research your trip adequately; any less than that and things get harried.

Decide How Many People Are Flying

If your twins are two years old or older, you will have to buy tickets for them. But babies and toddlers younger than two can fly for free if they sit on your lap. If you have two adults traveling, then both twins can be so-called "lap children" and you'll only have to buy two tickets. But be aware that you may not be able to fly by yourself with your twins. Although technically an adult can fly with one child in her lap if the other child has his own seat, many airlines stipulate that an adult can only travel with one infant. For all practical purposes, you may be forced to fly with another adult if you want to take your twins.

Buy Tickets for Everyone on International Flights

If you're flying internationally, you won't want to skimp on seats, even if you have infants who can be held on your lap. Children receive reduced fares on international flights (usually a 50 percent discount), so you should absolutely book seats for them. This is the time to book your children's meals, too.

See What Your Airline Offers and Request It

Some airlines offer bassinets on international or transcontinental flights, but you need to request them at the time you book your tickets. You should also find out if changing stations are available and where the bathrooms are located in relation to your seats.

Call the Airline to Check If Your Car Seat Will Fit

Depending on the size of the airplane, some car seats fit better than others. Smaller planes, for example, may not accommodate larger car seats. Even if you prefer to book your tickets online, it pays to call the airline and clarify the kind of aircraft generally used for the flight you want to take and whether your specific car seat will fit.

Arrange for Car Seats at Your Destination

If your twins are young enough to use car seats and you plan on taking them on the plane, then you're assured of having car seats at your destination.

However, if your twins will be "lap children" on the flight and you don't want to lug car seats along with the other mounds of equipment you'll need, you will want to arrange for car seats at your destination. There are multiple options. If you're renting a car, the rental company may offer car seats for an additional daily or weekly fee. You can also rent car seats through specialized baby-equipment rental companies (see the tip in "Plan for Your Arrival," below). Finally, check with relatives to see if they, or anyone they know, have car seats that you can borrow when you arrive. The downside of renting or borrowing car seats is that you'll have to be extra diligent in getting information on exactly the kind of car seat you'll get and, of course, there's no guarantee that you will get the kind of car seat you think is safest.

Plan for Your Arrival

Car seats are just one of the items you may need at your destination. How about cribs, Pack 'n Plays, bassinets, or high chairs? Because bringing everything you may need will be next to impossible (yes, I am checking fifteen pieces of luggage for a three-day trip), you will have to find a source for these items at your destination. Because I always relied on the good nature and scrounging skills of my family and friends, I was very surprised to learn there are rental companies that specialize in baby equipment and can provide everything you might need, from cribs and high chairs to Exersaucers, baby swings, and strollers. These companies range from franchises, like Baby's Away and the Traveling Baby Company, to small businesses that serve local areas, like Nana Enterprises in Maui, Hawaii. A simple Internet search for "baby equipment rentals" should bring you a lot of hits. Most states have one or several companies that serve the area, although you'll find more options in popular vacation areas, particularly those with a significant presence of vacation rental homes.

Go by Van

The amount of stuff you'll need for a trip with your twins will quickly overwhelm a standard-size car, and unless you can convince someone to drive you in his or her van or serve as a chauffeur for yours, probably the easiest thing to do is to order a taxi van. Unlike a regular taxi, a van will provide enough space for you to store all of your baggage, plus strap in your car seats. Since many taxi companies don't guarantee the kind of vehicle you will get, be sure to tell them you want a van. Also tell them the number of people and the number of bags (counting your car seats) you will have, to illustrate just why you need that van.

Take Advantage of the Extra Carry-On Baggage Allowance

Generally, the "one carry-on item" restriction allows you to carry a diaper bag in addition to your regular carry-on bag, regardless of whether your baby has a ticket or sits on your lap.

Pack Strategically

When packing, opt for bags with multiple access points and sealed compartments so that if something spills, the damage is minimal or, if you have to reach in and get something specific, you can put your hand on it right away. This is one of the reasons I recommend backpacks over diaper bags. Also, make liberal use of plastic and mesh bags to group things like changing supplies or toys together. In addition, if two adults are traveling and will be sitting apart from each other, make sure you take two separate bags or backpacks full of baby-related stuff and stock them similarly. It can be a real hassle if the twin you are holding needs to be changed but the diapers are all packed in the bag your spouse has two rows in front of you.

AT THE AIRPORT

Navigating security, long lines, and the endless trek to your gate doesn't have to be an exercise in physical and emotional stamina. Allow yourself extra time to get to your gate, and use items that will help you transport your gear and enable others to help you.

Bring Birth Certificates and Other Emergency Information

Bring photocopies of your babies' birth certificates, as well as your insurance information, the name and phone number of your babies' doctor, and emergency contacts both locally and at your destination. Although it's unlikely that you'll actually need all of this information, it's helpful to have in case of emergency or even if one of your twins is sick. Make two copies, and be sure both adults pack this information in separate bags in case your luggage gets lost or delayed. Note that if you're flying internationally, your twins—even infants—will need passports.

Use Separate Umbrella Strollers

Airport security lines tend to snake along narrow paths, security checkpoint gates are fairly narrow, and airports tend to be very crowded. Even if you've got a perfectly good double umbrella stroller at home, pony up and buy two separate ones for air travel purposes.

Use a Backpack

Backpacks are ideally suited for the airport for multiple reasons. First, they can be crammed with essentials; second, they are easier to carry than rolling carry-on bags or traditional diaper bags; and finally, they leave your hands free for carrying your twins or pushing a stroller. If your twins are older, consider investing in baby backpack carriers.

Allow Extra Time to Go Through Airport Security

The airport security process is quite laborious with twins and all their gear. Don't underestimate the amount of time you'll need. When you're juggling two babies and perhaps a toddler, it can take as much as ten minutes just to load your bags onto the conveyer, take off your shoes and coat, fold down the strollers, take off backpacks and baby holders, undress or unwrap your babies, go through security, then repeat the entire process in reverse. Ignore the dirty looks from other passengers. You need the extra time; they should have picked a line that moved faster.

Dress Your Babies with Airport Security in Mind

Airport security personnel will ask you to take off your own coat and shoes and your babies' items, too. Dress your babies in socks only, or have them wear slip-on shoes instead of shoes that tie or have straps. And make sure you unswaddle your babies before you go through security.

Don't Count on Preboarding

Preboarding used to be a given for passengers who needed more time to get to their seats and settle in, especially families with small children. But if you've traveled in coach in recent years you know that so-called standard amenities are no longer standard. This is why it's important to streamline the amount of baggage you have and become supermobile: Pack well, pack light, and bring wheels. The last thing you need while trying to carry two babies is a mound of luggage, a slew of bags, and a double stroller.

Engage the Gate Staff

Don't sit far away from the gate staff in the waiting area, especially if you have babies or toddlers. Sit close and leverage the cuteness or sympathy factor by letting the airline gate staff see you and your babies. You want them to be aware that you may need extra help boarding, or that they need to alert the flight staff that you are traveling with twins. A little positive attention can go a long way. Conversely, a little negative attention, such as being rude or extremely demanding, can hurt you. Act accordingly.

Gate-Check Your Strollers

You can drive your twins right up to the airplane door in a stroller, where someone will check it for you. Check in with the staff when you get to the gate, though, so they can ticket your stroller.

ON THE FLIGHT

Thoughtful packing, good seating arrangements, and a positive attitude can make or break the flight for you and those around you.

Make Friends with the Flight Attendants

Flight attendants can really help make the flight an easier, more pleasant experience for you and your family. They can facilitate how and when you board, run interference with other passengers, warm up the babies' formula, or bring extra blankets. But to make them go that extra mile on your behalf, endeavor to be friendly. Make eye contact and schmooze them. You want the attendants to realize that helping you is a positive thing, instead of dreading the fact that you are on board their flight.

Bring Car Seats Just in Case

Even if your babies will sit on your lap(s) during the flight, bring car seats. If your flight isn't full, the flight attendants will allow you to install them in empty seats, even though you haven't paid for them. If the plane is full, they will check them at the gate.

Pack Multiple "Quick Meal" Bags

If you are bottle-feeding, prepare and pack "quick meal" bags with formula, extra nipples (in case the ones you are using get clogged), and wipes. I used to pack these items into small insulated bags along with some ice packs and stash them in the seat pocket in front of me. I'd also pack extras in my diaper bags. When the babies were hungry, the bottle of formula was right there at my fingertips, at which point I could just hand it to the flight attendant to warm up.

Bring a Cover-Up

If you're breast-feeding, pack a small blanket or cover-up in your carry-on, then slip it into the seat pocket in front of you as you sit down. Even if you're sitting in the window seat with your baby, someone will notice you breast-feeding and will be unduly curious or offended. While I fully support a woman's right to breast-feed her baby in public if she needs to, I also remember

feeling very uncomfortable when people walking down the aisle seemed mes-
merized by the sight of me discreetly (always completely covered) breast-
feeding my daughter.

Pack Multiple "Quick Change" Bags

Pack a few large Ziploc freezer bags with a diaper, a few wipes, and some
diaper cream if necessary. You can slip one or two into each of the seat
pockets in front of you so that you have easy access to much-needed supplies
during the flight. This prevents you from having to lug an entire diaper bag
along with your baby as you walk to the airplane bathroom, and from having
to dig in your diaper bag in the tight quarters of an airplane seat section,
aisle, or bathroom.

Pack Extra Earplugs

If you're worried that your babies will cry and disturb the other passengers,
purchase some extra earplugs and offer them to the people around you. It
makes for a nice gesture and may help win over some of the folks around
you, so they'll be more forgiving of your having to travel with crying infants
or toddlers, especially if you're on a long flight.

Bring Pacifiers or Bottles

Young children may experience ear pain when the plane ascends during take-
off and descends during the landing. Using a pacifier or a bottle may alleviate
this pain. Older children may benefit from chewing gum or gummy snacks.

Pack Snacks

Cheerios, raisins, or small crackers work well. Pack extra, because they will
surely be dropped or spilled.

Bring Something to Cuddle

Your twins may want a blanket or stuffed animal to cuddle with and make
them feel more comfortable. Don't forget to pack these special items.

Bring Toys and Surprises

With older twins, boredom may be your worst battle. Bring both familiar
and some new toys to occupy your children. If your twins tend to fight over
toys, make sure you bring two of each item to reduce fighting and tears
(yours!).

Tether the Toys

Although your babies or toddlers will love playing with the toys that you
bring on the plane, they will also drop or throw them repeatedly. Rather than

spend the entire time trying to retrieve them, you can attach a long string or cord to the toy. This way you can pull it back up when it falls or, if it gets stuck on something, you'll be able to locate where it got stuck. (I've spent nearly entire flights bending over to look under seats trying to find the elusive toy my kids dropped.) Probably the easiest thing to do is to duct tape a string or cord onto larger toys. (It also works great with keys and rattles.) For coloring books, I would sometimes use a hole punch to create a hole through which I could thread some butcher's twine or plastic cord from the craft store. My goal was simply to have a way to easily retrieve dropped toys.

Seat Your Twins Strategically

With older twins, have one child sit in back of the other. That way, at least one child's kicking is confined to another child's seat, not a fellow passenger's seat.

Bring a Towel and Change of Clothing for Each Child

Airplanes are crowded, which will guarantee that you, your partner, or one of your twins will spill something. The tight quarters will also seemingly guarantee that your normally sweet-smelling babies will have smelly or leaking diapers that will have neighboring passengers shooting you dirty looks before the plane even takes off. Airplanes also tend to pump cold air just when you dress your babies for hot weather. For these reasons, take a change of clothes for each of your twins, and bring a towel for that spill just waiting to happen.

WHEN TRAVELING WITH CAR SEATS

Using car seats in a plane introduces a whole extra set of concerns, most of which can be worked out in advance.

Avoid Booking Seats in the Bulkhead or the Back Row

Your babies' car seats will not fit in all rows. For example, armrests in the bulkhead rows are stationary and can't be lifted to accommodate the car seat, and the last row doesn't recline and can make car seat installation very difficult.

Choose the Window and Middle Seats

Most airlines require your car seat to be installed in the window seat (in smaller planes) or the center seat (in larger planes). Car seats are not permitted in aisle seats.

Let One Person Install the Car Seats First

If possible, have one person board earlier and install the car seats (and put away the carry-on luggage and diaper bags, of course) while the other waits with the twins right outside the airplane door. Then, after installing the seats, your partner can either come and get you or have a flight attendant inform you that the seats are ready.

Install Seats Based on Your Child's Age and Weight

Use your car seats in an airplane in the same way they'd be used in a car: rear-facing for babies younger than a year old and under twenty pounds, front-facing for children at least a year old and weighing more than twenty pounds. (Although installing car seats in the rear-facing position is considered safer and is actually recommended for children up to thirty-five pounds, this may not be a comfortable option for your children on an airplane where space is at a premium.)

Book Seats in Rows One Behind the Other

Sitting across the aisle from each other may seem like a good idea, but it's not. If you take car seats on the plane, it's unlikely both of you will be sitting in the aisle seats, so you will probably have one or even two people, plus an aisle, between you and your traveling partner. Instead, plan to sit in two separate rows, one behind the other. This makes it easier to coordinate how you care for the twins because it allows you to easily hand over toys, foods, or diapers (or even exchange babies) if necessary. It also allows you to play peekaboo with your older twins and limits the noise and distractions to one small area.

Avoid Other Restraint Devices

Most airlines prohibit so-called "belly belts," which are vests worn by your children that are secured to the airplane seat belts and vests or harnesses that hold the baby to the adult's chest. Don't spend your money on these items, even if their manufacturers advertise that the products can be used on airplanes. They usually can't.

GREAT TRAVEL GEAR

Some items just make your travel experience hundreds of times better.

Buy a Wheelie Car Seat Travel Bag by The Right Start

This heavy-duty nylon bag allows you to protect and carry your car seat during travel. The bonus is that it has wheels on the bottom and a shoulder strap, so the car seat is super easy to carry.

Buy a gogo Kidz Travelmate

This is a fabulous product that allows you to wheel your car seat with your child still in it. Essentially it turns your car seat into a rolling piece of luggage. The Travelmate is a car seat attachment with a handle and wheels. It weighs about five pounds, the handle telescopes up easily, and one person can easily pull two car seats with children inside while the other manages the remaining gear.

Use Stroller Connectors

If you are using two separate umbrella strollers (as recommended previously) in order to have greater versatility in crowded spaces, there may still be times that only one person is available to push both strollers. In those instances, you can attach a pair of molded plastic stroller connectors that turn the two strollers into a double stroller. The connectors are inexpensive (retailing for about $12) and very small and easy to carry in your purse or backpack. You'll find they come in very handy.

Have Crib Toys with Velcro

For young children, crib toys that are soft, chewable, and come with Velcro strips are the perfect airplane toys. These toys are also incorporated into baby play mats, so I used to raid the play mats we had at home when we needed to travel rather than going out and buying new toys.

Bring Along Travel-Size Packets of Pain Relievers

For you and your impending headache. Enough said.

14

Vacationing with Your Children

One of the ironies of being the parent of twins is that while they make you need a vacation even more, they also make it more difficult for you to actually take one. You end up paying more, taking more stuff, and working harder when you should be relaxing. Parents of twins should opt for places where they can spread out and where their children will feel comfortable. Generally, vacation means renting a house or a hotel suite and finding some childcare so that mom and dad can get some time off from constant parenting. And when vacationing, it pays to pare down to the essentials. Leave the giant stroller and oversize toys behind when you head for the beach or the mountains. Younger twins will benefit from the change of scenery, too, as long as some of their basic routines remain unchanged. If you plan your vacation to accommodate your large family and pack with a vacation in mind, you can have a great time. Here are some things to consider.

Planning Your Vacation
✓ Match your vacation to your twins' age.
✓ Pick nonpeak vacation periods.
✓ Go for at least a week if you're flying.
✓ Vacation locally.
✓ Rent a house.
✓ Target family-friendly resorts.
✓ Delve beyond the marketing hype.
✓ Decide if you want an all-inclusive arrangement.
✓ Get advice from those who've been there.

✓ Search out "family of five" or "big family" specials.

✓ Remember that car seats are not the rule everywhere.

Tips to Make Your Trip Smoother

✓ Take along an international cell phone.

✓ Leave the giant stroller at home.

✓ Pack only a handful of toys, and pick them according to your destination.

✓ Practice before you leave.

✓ Don't expect your twins to share a bed easily.

✓ Stick to a schedule.

✓ Guard the bed.

✓ Use crib sheets from home in the babies' cribs.

✓ Pack insulated bags and Ziploc Baggies.

✓ Bring a Thermos.

✓ Use diapers as packing material and buy more on-site.

✓ Use bottled water for formula.

✓ Bring masking tape.

✓ Bring some detergent.

✓ Bring a portable DVD player and some DVDs.

If You Choose a Hotel

✓ Opt for suites or connecting rooms.

✓ Check out the room layout in advance.

✓ Get a room on the ground floor.

✓ Pack your own snacks.

✓ Carry wipes and Baggies everywhere.

If You Choose a House

✓ Rent your baby equipment.

✓ Find babysitters.

✓ Bring or rent a beach cabana or beach umbrellas.

PLANNING YOUR VACATION

Family-friendly travel is a huge business, so you should have a lot of options in terms of where to go. But remember that twins need some special considerations, especially given all of the gear they require.

Match Your Vacation to Your Twins' Age

When planning your vacation, keep in mind the age of your twins. Babies will be pretty happy anywhere, and young children tend to be happiest as long they have some daily activities and some space to run around and play, which makes beach vacations a great pick. If you want to do an activity-centered vacation, such as Disney World or a water park, wait until your children are older, at least five or six, so they can enjoy the rides and you don't have to carry all the gear babies require. For these reasons, you may find yourself going to Mexico or the Caribbean with your babies, but Florida and other U.S.-based destinations with school-age children. Save camping, sightseeing, and sports- and adventure-oriented vacations for older kids.

Pick Nonpeak Vacation Periods

Not surprisingly, flights, hotels, and resorts get booked up when the weather is best and kids and their parents are out of school and work. Accordingly, if you want more flexibility in terms of flights, as well as lower prices, avoid traveling during school breaks (Christmas/winter break, Easter/spring break, and the height of summer). Good times to travel with small children include May and September. During both months the weather tends to be nice, but older kids are either still in or going back to school. Some resorts even offer price discounts for families with young children in September.

Go for at Least a Week If You're Flying

If you're flying to your destination, you're better off booking a vacation that's at least a week long. Although you may think a short trip is easier on your twins, remember that there's a significant amount of disruption in the process of flying (or going on a long drive, for that matter), and by the time you're done packing and traveling your twins will need some time to unwind and acclimate. If your trip is only three or four days long, you'll be headed home just as your babies are adjusting to their new environment.

Vacation Locally

It may not be as exotic as a beach vacation in Mexico, but you can get plenty of relaxation by renting a house in a resort area within driving distance. Not only will you save money by not having to buy airline tickets, but you will have much more space to accommodate your twins and their baby gear, plus you'll be close enough to return home quickly in case of emergency.

Rent a House

For families with twins, rental houses are the way to go. At a hotel, unless you rent a large suite, you're pretty much limited to one or two rooms, usually without a kitchen. And if your children are young, they probably have early bedtimes, which means that you will also be forced to retire early and stay quiet in your small space so the kids can fall asleep. In contrast, many rental houses offer great amenities both inside and out, with pools and easy access to the beach. One summer, when our twins were smaller, we rented a house that was a short walk from some beautiful beaches on Lake Michigan, but that also had a pool and a huge yard for our kids. Frankly, all three of our children enjoyed the house amenities more than the beach itself. Another time, we rented a house on the beach in Connecticut. The house was extremely modest, but it offered a great backyard, lovely views, and a phenomenal kid-friendly beach right outside our door. You can easily rent homes not only in the United States, but in well-known beach resort destinations in Mexico and the Caribbean, too. Check out some websites, including Vacationrentals.com and, for a listing of vacation rentals by owner, VRBO.com.

Target Family-Friendly Resorts

If you're interested in a beach vacation, Jamaica, the Dominican Republic, and Mexico are among the top budget-friendly choices for families. There are numerous resorts that cater to families by offering kids' clubs, childcare, and babysitting services. Also, if you opt for a family resort, you and your family will find a better fit in terms of activities and environment than at resorts frequented by couples or single adults.

Delve Beyond the Marketing Hype

For many parents, the appeal of a family-friendly resort is the childcare options they offer. Parents want a vacation where they can relax for several hours knowing that their children are being well cared for. But finding this level of service can be a problem for families traveling with very small children. Even if resorts sell themselves as family-friendly, not all offer activities or day care for infants and toddlers. Some resorts only accept children three or five years old and older. This information is often buried on the resort's website, so be sure to seek it out. You can also contact the resort directly to get clarification on its childcare policy and costs. Then, armed with this knowledge, you can go ahead and book the vacation through the travel agency offering that great low rate.

Decide If You Want an All-Inclusive Arrangement

Many resorts catering to families are all-inclusive, with all of your meals and drinks covered under the cost. Beyond the cost savings, the upside to all-inclusives is convenience and choice. You don't have to cook and there are plenty of meal options to choose from. The caveat is that the meals are not necessarily kid-friendly. Too often, meals for children consist of a limited menu of chicken fingers, pizza, pasta, hot dogs, and fries, which is not the healthiest diet for any child. Even if your kids love all of these foods, they may balk at having the same things every day for lunch and dinner for seven or ten days running. In contrast, you can provide better food choices if you decide to cook for yourselves, but this means finding a resort that is close to a town and that offers a kitchen or kitchenette. Families with twins will have to weigh the benefit of built-in childcare against the benefit of better and more varied food choices and more space to spread out.

Get Advice from Those Who've Been There

There are some excellent travel websites where you can find reviews and advice from other travelers. Tripadvisor.com is an excellent site where you can search for comments and feedback on hotels, resorts, and overall destinations. Travelers write about their experiences, offer tips, and even post photos of their trip—and they don't hold back, whether raving about great experiences or criticizing their negative ones. Other good websites include www .familytravelboards.com and www.travelwithkids.com.

Search Out "Family of Five" or "Big Family" Specials

If you have twins plus another child, your options for travel packages narrow. Hotels usually allow only two adults and two children in a room, so families with three small children who can't be in a separate room alone are limited to more expensive options, such as renting suites if they want to stay in a resort. Work with a travel agency that specializes in family travel, or specifically search for resorts that cater to bigger families. These hotels offer villas or suites with two or three bedrooms; some are also all-inclusive. There are multiple options in Mexico (including Cancún, Riviera Maya, Puerto Vallarta, and Los Cabos); Jamaica; the Dominican Republic (both in Punta Cana and La Romana); and Hawaii.

Remember That Car Seats Are Not the Rule Everywhere

You've lugged the two car seats from your home to the airport and onto the plane, headed to some gorgeous Caribbean destination. But as you get into a taxi or a transport van to take you to your hotel or rental house, you realize there's no way to install the seats, or that there aren't even any seat belts. In fact, unless you plan on renting a car, you may not be able to install infant or child car seats. Have your hotel or resort put you in touch with the transport company it uses and check to see if car seats are used or can be installed in their vehicles. Transport vans are more likely to accommodate car seats than regular taxis.

TIPS TO MAKE YOUR TRIP SMOOTHER

The best advance planning can't cover every contingency, but the following tips should help minimize the disruptions inherent in a new environment.

Take Along an International Cell Phone

Your regular cell phone won't work abroad, so either rent a phone or buy a subscriber identity module (SIM) card that enables your phone to make and receive international calls. Be sure you know and test the phone's features before you leave, and bring extra copies of the instructions in case you forget how it works. Bring an adapter, too, so you can charge the phone. In general, having a cell phone provides peace of mind. If you're going on a longer trip or know that you and your partner will be separated during the trip, buy or rent two phones so that you can contact each other on-site.

Leave the Giant Stroller at Home

Your vacation will go a lot more smoothly the less you have to worry about carting stuff around. Double strollers, though convenient at home, are a pain to travel with. Choose some lightweight umbrella strollers with sunshades and bring a couple of plastic stroller connectors in case you want to turn the single strollers into a double stroller.

Pack Only a Handful of Toys, and Pick Them According to Your Destination

You should definitely bring some toys for your twins, but you don't have to bring the entire contents of your house. If you're going to the beach, bring beach toys that can be left behind if necessary. Avoid larger battery-operated toys and opt for coloring books, blocks, or stuffed animals instead—things that are easy to transport and that rely on your children's imagination to keep them occupied.

Practice Before You Leave

When traveling, one of the biggest changes your babies or toddlers will have to adjust to is the different sleeping environment on vacation. Let your babies "practice" by having them sleep in a Pack 'n Play before you go on vacation. A girlfriend of mine said that the unfamiliar environment was so disruptive for her one-year-old twins that she could not sleep for all their antics and crying, while her husband left the hotel room and retreated to the car so that he could get some sleep.

Don't Expect Your Twins to Share a Bed Easily

There's nothing wrong with expecting your twins to share the same bed while on vacation, but it may not go smoothly if they tend to disrupt each other. At home, have them share the same room (if they don't already) and have them practice sleeping in the same bed for a night or two before you book your trip. This process will help you determine if they can handle it, if they need more practice, or if you should just go ahead and book two separate rooms.

Stick to a Schedule

Whether you're staying in a hotel or a house, the best way to let your kids adjust to their new surroundings is to stick to your normal schedule. If possible, feed and bathe your twins at the same time you normally would and impose a strict bedtime.

Guard the Bed

Toddlers who still sleep in cribs at home may be able to sleep together on a full-size or queen-size bed as long as you minimize their chances of falling out of bed. You can purchase and bring bed rails (although they can be bulky to transport) or use specially designed inflatable bolster pillows. These pillows attach to the bed mattress and are sold under the brand names BedBugz Bed Bolster (by ToddlerCoddler) or Bed Bolster to Go (sold by One Step Ahead).

One solution that we've used is to push the bed against the wall, then stack our suitcases by the open side and cover them with extra pillows, blankets, and clothes to make a soft landing spot in case one of our twins should roll off (they did, and it worked). One thing to note: Bed rails should not be used with infants, who should always sleep in cribs, bassinets, or Pack 'n Plays, lest they become trapped between the rails and the mattress.

Use Crib Sheets from Home in the Babies' Cribs

Even if the cribs they're using are different, your babies will feel more at home sleeping on their own crib sheets. Launder them in your usual detergent so the babies experience a familiar smell. For older children, bring pillows and pillowcases from home for the same purpose.

Pack Insulated Bags and Ziploc Baggies
Use the insulated bags to store formula and cool them with baggies filled with hotel ice. It's a handy way to bring along formula if you feed the babies outside your room or decide to go sightseeing.

Bring a Thermos
A Thermos filled with hot water makes a great bottle warmer; it also allows you to make feedings more portable.

Use Diapers as Packing Material and Buy More On-Site
Your twins will go through *a lot* of diapers on a vacation, and of course you'll need some for the times you're actually traveling. Although your best bet is to buy diapers when you arrive on-site, that may not be practical if you're going somewhere remote. Pack the equivalent of at least one large package of diapers into your suitcase, tucking them loosely into empty spaces. Then, upon your arrival, take a taxi to a local store and stock up on the local brand.

Use Bottled Water for Formula
You can't really count on the quality of the water if you're going on vacation, and if you're staying in a hotel, boiled water may be impossible to come by. Instead, buy sealed bottles of water and use them to mix formula that you bring from home.

Bring Masking Tape
Masking tape lets you easily baby-proof all the electrical outlets in your lodgings. It's especially helpful to have on hand if you are somewhere outside of the United States and the electrical plugs are shaped differently and you don't want to have to buy special safety plugs. You can also use masking tape to tape shut cabinet doors you don't want your twins to open.

Bring Some Detergent
Your kids will get their clothes dirty. Instead of trying to clean them with bath or hand soap, bring a small amount of powered detergent to wash their (and possibly your) clothes.

Bring a Portable DVD Player and Some DVDs
Hotels may have great amenities, but rarely do they offer lots of kid-themed television programming. And although you may wonder why you should even think about movies and television with the great pools and beaches, activities, and sightseeing outside, small children will want some downtime

and a retreat from all the new surroundings. Watching favorite movies or programs will calm them and make them feel more at home. Just don't forget the adapter if you plan on leaving the States.

IF YOU CHOOSE A HOTEL

You'll want to choose a hotel with great amenities and low rates, of course, but you also want to make sure you have enough room to spread out.

Opt for Suites or Connecting Rooms

Some larger hotel rooms offer an alcove or a large closet where you can put a crib or Pack 'n Play. Large rooms with alcoves may be more appropriate if your twins are small enough to sleep together or can sleep in Pack 'n Plays, but connecting rooms work better for older twins.

Check Out the Room Layout in Advance

If you all room together, try to get the room layout in advance so that you can see the placement and general size of the sleeping area. We discovered the importance of this the hard way: When we vacationed with our oldest daughter, her crib was in an alcove that also happened to be right by the sliding glass door to the balcony. This was an awkward setup because it made it difficult for us to get out of the room and sit on the balcony without disturbing her. The proximity of the alcove to the sliding doors also meant we were exposed to the noise from the band outside (which played for several hours every night), so it was as loud as if she were sleeping outside as well. Needless to say, it was more stressful than we anticipated trying to make sure that she slept.

Get a Room on the Ground Floor

Avoid rooms where you have to climb a lot of stairs if your twins are small and you have to carry them. Also, the layout of many resorts features multiple small buildings clustered around a pool or near an outdoor restaurant. If you are in a ground-floor room, you can relax outside on your balcony or just outside the sliding glass doors and still feel like you're mingling with other adults while your twins sleep. You're not quite as removed from everything as you would be on a higher floor.

Pack Your Own Snacks

All-inclusive hotel resorts may offer plenty of foods, but they typically don't offer any snack foods suitable for small children. You may luck out at breakfast, where cold cereal and possibly raisins are available, but good luck finding snack foods at other times of the day. Bring along your Ziploc baggies and stash some cereal for snacking later in the day.

Carry Wipes and Baggies Everywhere

We were never the type of parents to obsessively clean off surfaces in stores or other public places, but all-inclusive resorts are an entirely different matter. You'll especially want to wipe down the cafeteria tables and chairs. With so many people eating in the main area, your twins can easily pick up germs from someone who is sick. (Imagine getting to your fabulous island destination, then having your kids pick up the stomach flu from someone on your second day there. That pretty much signals the end of your vacation.) In addition, cleaning up after your twins is a must, and wipes will do a tremendous job. Baggies are perfect for carrying a small number of wipes or holding a small stash of crackers or cereal, and if they're larger, Baggies are useful for sealing in dirty diapers until you can dispose of them.

IF YOU CHOOSE A HOUSE

A rental house is ideal for larger families, and with these tips you can make it feel more like a homey vacation.

Rent Your Baby Equipment

Since rental homes allow you more room to spread out, you may want or need more baby equipment than at a hotel. For example, most hotels provide high chairs in their restaurants, but you would need to get your own if you're renting a house. Baby-equipment rental companies operate in many resort areas and cater to families in rental homes. Many of these companies will deliver and also set up cribs, high chairs, and other equipment so you don't have to.

Find Babysitters

If you're renting a house with another family, you can each trade off nights to serve as babysitters for each other's kids. Your extended family can also pitch in if you're visiting family members. But if your family is traveling alone, you are not necessarily doomed to spend every night at home. Get babysitter recommendations from the homeowners you're renting from, or if you're traveling in the United States, try www.sittercity.com to find babysitters at your destination. Contact potential babysitting candidates just as soon as you arrive so that you can interview them, check references, and get them familiar with your children. Have your potential sitters stay for several hours while you're with them, so you can see how they interact with and care for your twins.

Bring or Rent a Beach Cabana or Beach Umbrellas

Perhaps your rental house stocks them; if not, buy or rent some beach umbrellas or a baby cabana, which are musts for your beach vacation.

PART FOUR

LIFE AFTER BABYHOOD

15

Keeping the Peace

L ife with twins is not all lollipops and sunshine. It also involves a lot of fighting, screaming, yelling, biting, pushing, and hair pulling. Though they may be best friends, your twins will also fight constantly and sometimes over the silliest things. They'll fight with each other and with their siblings, too. Among twins, it's also pretty common for one twin to be more dominant and pushy while the other is more laid-back and easygoing, which can exacerbate sharing issues. As the parent, you can either play the constant referee or you can develop an arsenal of tricks to mediate their fights and help your twins learn to share and, when necessary, to speak up for themselves. But first, you have to lay the groundwork for sharing and decide which items are worth buying in doubles and which aren't. Here are some helpful suggestions.

Laying the Groundwork
✓ Find the root of the sharing problems.
✓ Teach and reinforce the concept of sharing.
✓ Read from children's books about sharing.
✓ Make some things off-limits.
✓ Be consistent.

Making Sharing Easy
✓ Build a stash of identical basics.
✓ Double up on small toys.
✓ Double up on toys that require extended play.
✓ Encourage the sharing of big toys.

✓ Make sure the toys are big enough for two.
✓ Be generous with big toy accessories.
✓ Buy different but similar toys.
✓ Label toys by child.
✓ Use name tags and monograms to label clothes.
✓ Buy multiple step stools for younger children.
✓ Buy toys that encourage cooperation.
✓ Organize your home.
✓ Put away special toys.

In the Heat of the Moment
✓ Put the toy in time-out.
✓ Set a time limit on toys.
✓ Use a timer.
✓ Redirect the twins' attention.
✓ Take one of the kids outside.
✓ Disrupt the environment.
✓ Count to ten.
✓ Nip dangerous or violent behavior in the bud.

Practicing How to Share and Take Turns
✓ Play a sharing game.
✓ Play a helper game.
✓ Have your twins exchange "gifts."
✓ Role-play with your children.
✓ Put sharing on a blackboard, sign, or chore chart.
✓ Avoid intervening in every situation.
✓ Observe your twins' personalities.
✓ Encourage time apart.
✓ Reward good behavior with praise and stickers.
✓ Practice taking turns.
✓ Emphasize each child's specialness to you.

LAYING THE GROUNDWORK

Unless you want to deal with nonstop fighting and crying, instill the importance of sharing as soon as your twins are old enough to understand what it means. But also remember that sharing everything all the time is too much to expect of anyone. Make sure your twins have things that are theirs alone.

Find the Root of the Sharing Problems

What's at the root of your twins' sharing issues? Little ones (toddlers through preschoolers), for example, may have a more difficult time sharing with their siblings because they have a tougher time expressing themselves than older children. Instead of asking for a toy, they'll just grab it away from their twin. And when someone grabs their toy, they'll bite and pull hair in retaliation. On the other hand, older twins may be so tired of feeling like one-half of a pair that they'll use whatever opportunities come their way to fight or to assert their own desires. If you can find out why sharing is a problem, then you can take concrete steps to work it out.

Teach and Reinforce the Concept of Sharing

Take opportunities to express how you and your spouse share. At dinner, point out how everyone shares the same food. When you're running an errand, explain how the family shares a car. Point out that sharing is both common and expected: "You're not the only ones who have to share a room. Mommy and Daddy share their room, too." Set the tone by making sharing a family issue, not just a kids' issue.

Read from Children's Books About Sharing

Books are a great way to reinforce the concept of sharing, especially for younger children. Some great titles on sharing include *Share and Take Turns* by Cheri J. Meiners and Meredith Johnson (Free Spirit Publishing), *Sharing Is Fun* by Joanna Cole and Maxie Chambliss (HarperCollins), *I Am Sharing* by Mercer Mayer (Random House Books for Young Readers), and *Twins Have a Fight* by Ellen Weiss and Sam Williams (Aladdin).

Make Some Things Off-Limits

Not everything should be up for sharing. Make sure each of your twins has some toys, plates, cups, and clothes that are his (or hers) alone. In our household, we try and share everything, but the twins and their older sister know that they all have things that they have a special claim to, and if their brother or sister is using it, it must be given up upon request. Often just knowing something is "theirs," and that they can ask for it back, makes our kids feel more generous about sharing their things.

Be Consistent

It's easy to talk about sharing when everyone is calm, but it's a different story when one of your twins is shrieking because her sister took her favorite doll away. It's important not to break down and give in to their demands when things get tough. If keeping the peace between your twins is your long-term goal, you have to be consistent in the short term. You'll be yelling "Share!" until your voice is hoarse.

MAKING SHARING EASY

Sharing is easier if there's enough to go around. While you don't have to have identical everything, you should have two of the more popular items.

Build a Stash of Identical Basics
There are some things your kids are just going to want to play with over and over again, and those are the items you want to have doubles of. Depending on the gender of your twins, you should have at least a couple of identical baby dolls, playground balls, buckets and shovels, tea sets, trucks, purses or backpacks, tractors, fire trucks, playground chalk, and doctor kits. This issue does not disappear with boy-girl twins: We have multiple doll strollers, bottles of bubbles, chairs, bears, and at least three tea sets, which are popular not only for play picnics but for pretend tea parties in the bathtub.

Double Up on Small Toys
Buy doubles of small toys. It makes no sense to get one truck or die-cast car if you know both of your boys are going to want to play with them at the same time. The same thing goes for Barbie dolls, necklaces, bracelets and rings, and balls.

Double Up on Toys That Require Extended Play
Similarly, make sure you buy doubles of toys that your children will use for extended play periods, such as coloring books, markers and crayons, buckets and shovels, and Leapster and Leap Pad games. It's also a good idea to get two sets of building blocks, because even though they can technically be shared (since they come in sets of multiples), if your set of blocks is fairly small, it will be harder for a child to play with a limited number of them.

Encourage the Sharing of Big Toys
Bigger toys, such as play kitchens, dollhouses, and puppet theaters, can easily be shared by two or even three children, and it's easier on your wallet than buying duplicates of these expensive toys. The only exception is bicycles and other sporting gear meant to be used by one child at a time. Buy a bike or a scooter for each child.

Make Sure the Toys Are Big Enough for Two

Sometimes a favorite toy is simply too small to share. Some toys need to be big enough for two. For example, when buying a play kitchen, make sure it's big enough for two toddlers to actually stand in front of and play together. Similarly, if you buy or make a tent or a playhouse in the backyard, make sure there's room enough for everyone to fit.

Be Generous with Big Toy Accessories

Even a small play kitchen can be fun for two or three children if everyone has an apron, pot, lids, spoons, and some pretend food to cook. Several children can also take turns with the puppet theater if they each have a puppet instead of having to share one.

Buy Different but Similar Toys

For some toys, you're better off buying things that are similar but not identical. For instance, having two backpacks, one in pink and one in purple, will help ensure your twins feel they're being treated equally without having to forgo individuality. Toys that are on the expensive side and those your twins play with occasionally but not religiously are also good choices for the different but similar strategy: Buy two different types of remote-controlled cars or two different games; get a Dora the Explorer oven and a Dora dollhouse.

As an example, here's a list of the toys we have at our home. The list is typical for parents who have twins plus another child. Note which items are single and which are multiples: We have six baby dolls (two identical), two identical Cabbage Patch dolls, and twelve Barbies (two identical), but two doll beds (one for each of the identical dolls), three different types of doll strollers (one for each of the kids), and one dollhouse (for all three to share). We have eight playground balls (including two purple balls, since it is the girls' favorite color), but one bat and Wiffle ball and one toddler basketball hoop, mostly because our kids don't play that often. We have one train and one train track, but about fifty small die-cast cars and two dozen construction vehicles, each one different. We have three similar tea sets but one play kitchen; one puppet theater with three store-bought puppets and several homemade ones; three kids' umbrellas, raincoats, and pairs of rain boots; three flashlights and three sleeping bags, but one tent. We have three different sets of blocks, three doctors' kits, but multiple musical instruments, each one different. We have one art easel, but countless notebooks and three large containers of crayons and markers. We have three backpacks and several dress-up outfits, including two identical Little Red Riding Hood capes and three cowgirl and cowboy costumes (plus two stick ponies and one rocking horse). We also have three bicycles, two scooters, and two "car" strollers.

When the twins were babies, we had two play mats, two Exersaucers, two mobiles, and two bouncy chairs, but one swing and one learning-block toy.

Label Toys by Child

It's surprising how fights over identical items dissipate when you point out that the toy is not one child's but his twin's. We put names on a lot of different toys, including coloring books, games, and cars, using masking tape to mark things that are hard to write on.

Use Name Tags and Monograms to Label Clothes

Twins often share clothes, either because their parents want them to dress alike or because they simply like and want the same things. But you can reduce arguments over what is whose by using name tags for items of clothing or by having things monogrammed. In our house, all of the kids have bathrobes and stools with their names on them; some dress-up clothes have initials sewn right onto them so that we can immediately determine their rightful owner; and any other popular personal item that comes with an option for monogramming gets one.

Buy Multiple Step Stools for Younger Children

Believe it or not, one of the biggest causes of fights in our house is the humble step stool. We ended up buying several and have them all over the house. But think about it—smaller children want to do a lot of things that their environment makes very difficult: teeth brushing, washing hands, reaching things on the counter, getting spoons and forks from drawers. Avoid fights by buying multiple stools.

Buy Toys That Encourage Cooperation

Be sure to buy games, puzzles, balls, and other hands-on toys with multiple pieces. These toys encourage cooperation and sharing, and they will make life easier for all concerned.

Organize Your Home

Sometimes sharing problems are exacerbated when your home is messy and chaotic. It won't matter if you have four of the same item if you can't find what you need, when you need it. Even if you're not exceptionally organized or you just don't have the time to be as organized as you'd like to be, keep toys under control and keep them in regular spots. Use bins to organize your kids' toys by type and designate a place where they live, so that even when things are at their most chaotic you can go to the "usual" spot and find that one elusive toy that's being fought over.

Put Away Special Toys

Some toys that are not meant for sharing should not be kept in common areas of the home. Instead, they remain in the twins' room, or in their cribs, and are played with under supervised circumstances, which reduces fighting and tears among the kids.

IN THE HEAT OF THE MOMENT

But what should you do if your twins are fighting and screaming right now? It depends on the age. You can usually redirect the attention of younger children, while older children may have to be separated, punished, and have their toys taken away.

Put the Toy in Time-Out

Remove the toy in question (rather than giving it to one child) and put it away until both can share. Sometimes you only have to take it away for five or ten minutes and then things calm down, or your twins will forget the item entirely. This may be the only solution when your twins are fighting because they have to have that particular toy at that particular moment, despite having an exact duplicate at their fingertips.

Set a Time Limit on Toys

Announce a time limit on a toy in dispute, allowing each of your twins to play with an item for a set period of, say, five minutes.

Use a Timer

Sometimes, just saying there's a limited time to play with a toy is not enough, and five minutes will seem like an eternity to your kids. To help your twins recognize when one child's turn is over and the next child's turn has begun, use an egg timer, a watch, or anything that beeps to mark turns.

Redirect the Twins' Attention

Small children can bite, pull, slap, and kick with the best of them. But, blissfully, they can also be easily distracted most of the time. When your twins fight or cry over a toy, or anything else for that matter, try redirecting their attention by offering a snack, a drink, or another toy.

Take One of the Kids Outside

My husband does this one a lot. When our twins fight, or when one of our twins fights with his or her older sister, he simply takes one of the kids outside and finds something to redirect his or her attention toward. Usually, we don't take the time to dress the kids before going outside. The point is to startle them and what better way to do that than to take them out of a warm house and into the cold air. In warmer weather, taking the kids outside becomes more about distraction. This is when we do take the time to put on jackets and shoes if necessary so that the kids can stay outside and play if they want to. It usually takes less than two minutes to restore calm among everyone.

Disrupt the Environment

You can bring a heated situation to an abrupt end by disrupting the environment. By this I mean you can turn on or turn up the music, turn on or turn off the TV, knock on the door, ring the doorbell, or turn the lights off. We've even blown bubbles during a fight. When you disrupt the environment unexpectedly, it usually stops the kids in their tracks, at least for a moment, which is enough to separate them and quiet them down.

Count to Ten

Avoid yanking a toy out of the hands of one child in order to give it to the other. Instead, announce that the child holding the item in question has five or ten seconds to hand it over to you, then do a countdown. At the end of the countdown say, "Please give me the toy" and take it. Once you have item in hand, wait another few seconds before giving it to your other child. Drawing out the process seems to defuse the tension a bit, as does having your child hand the item to you rather than to his sibling.

Nip Dangerous or Violent Behavior in the Bud

Hair pulling, biting, pushing, and scratching all deserve a quick and firm "No!" If the behavior persists, don't be afraid to step in. One mom actually used a bit of soap in her girls' mouths, reasoning that although it might seem cruel, it had an immediate effect but did not hurt them. While I'm not recommending this particular strategy, sometimes you have to be firm or the behavior will escalate. When it comes to unacceptable behavior, most parents separate their twins, use time-outs, or take away privileges. In our household, favorite blankets and toys get taken away for a set period of time and the kids sit in time-outs.

PRACTICING HOW TO SHARE AND TAKE TURNS

As they say, practice makes perfect. If you incorporate sharing and taking turns into simple games, after a while the concept sticks, even for the smallest children. Reward good behavior and encourage time apart so that your twins have a little breathing space.

Play a Sharing Game

Have your small children sit in a circle and practice holding and passing a toy like a ball, a doll, or a truck. After a few seconds, announce, "Emma's turn," or "Mommy's turn," and have your child pass the item along. Keep the game going for several rounds. Have your children announce when it's their turn as well, in order to help them develop the confidence to both voice their desire for an object and to stand up for themselves if their more demanding sibling suddenly wants to grab the toy out of their hands.

Play a Helper Game

Have one child act as a helper. During playtime, for example, have one of your twins hand toys to her sister or brother. This strategy also works in the context of chores, such as when you're making dinner.

Have Your Twins Exchange "Gifts"

Have your twins each wrap a toy of theirs as a "gift" and give it to their sibling to play with for one week (or one day, if your twins are very young). You can keep the gift exchange going indefinitely, and you can adapt the idea to get the twins to share the most popular toys or the ones that cause the most fights.

Role-Play with Your Children

Ask your children what they say when they want to share. Ask them what they do when someone takes a toy away from them that they were playing with. Another version is the "It's Not Fair" game: Ask your children to finish the sentence, "It's not fair when . . ."

Put Sharing on a Blackboard, Sign, or Chore Chart

Remind your twins to share by writing it on a blackboard, making a sign, or putting it on a chore chart. It will seem more concrete once it's written down.

Avoid Intervening in Every Situation

It's hard not to step in when your twins are pulling and tugging at each other, but sometimes it's just better to let them work it out on their own. Try not to step in unless they're hurting each other.

Observe Your Twins' Personalities

In many families with twins, one child tends to be more dominant, while the other gives way to his brother or sister more frequently. Watch how your children interact and encourage your less dominant child to speak up for himself. When interrupting their arguments, however, take care not to always speak up on behalf of the more laid-back child. Just because one of your twins is pushier does not mean you don't have to stand up for him occasionally. Be fair to both of them.

Encourage Time Apart

Sometimes sharing becomes an issue because your twins spend all of their time together. Give your twins some time to be apart from each other and let them spend some time playing alone. And just as important, give each of your twins one-on-one time with you. If it's not required all of the time, sharing becomes easier.

Reward Good Behavior with Praise and Stickers

Not only is it important to praise and reward sharing, but you want to do it in a way that doesn't subvert your goal. Reward sharing and other good behaviors with praise and stickers or stars rather than with special treats such as candy. Letting one child "earn" or accumulate more toys than her sibling only fuels disparity.

Practice Taking Turns

There are multiple opportunities throughout the day to take turns. Have your twins alternate choosing books to read, or being the one who helps you stir cocoa into the milk or mix the cake batter, or sitting next to you on the sofa, or picking a movie to watch. For older kids, designate one night where each twin gets to choose what's for dinner. In the long run, keeping the peace between your twins is not necessarily about having or doing identical things, but about having equal opportunities and fairness.

Emphasize Each Child's Specialness to You

Sometimes kids don't want to hear that you love them all the same or equally. They want to feel they are important as individuals. For example, in the case of our oldest daughter, she would constantly ask me if we loved her more than the twins, and saying that we loved everyone the same didn't seem to help her feel better. So I came up with the idea to tell her I loved her first, because she was born first. Now she has a special claim: The twins may get more of my attention sometimes, and I don't love any child more than another, but I did love her first. And she smiles any time I tell her that.

16

Baby-Proofing Your Home

Perhaps the biggest difference parents of twins have to contend with when thinking about baby-proofing is the "monkey see, monkey do" factor. Unlike singletons, twins can work together to circumvent the most secure baby-proofing devices. In the few minutes your back is turned, they'll open heavy refrigerator doors, climb onto each other to reach high objects, and drag chairs across the room and jointly push closed doors ajar. Oh, and in case you thought that wasn't enough, they'll egg each other on in a competitive way, slam doors on each other's fingers, and even if one is being good, chances are the other is getting into something he shouldn't. So you need to baby-proof accordingly, not only covering all of the basics recommended to parents of singletons, but going that extra step to help secure the house against your twin terrors . . . er, children. Here are some suggestions for tackling every area of your home.

The Fundamentals
✓ Deal with the basics first.

The Kitchen
✓ Double up on door locks.
✓ Use a combination lock if necessary.
✓ Buy low stools.
✓ Install extra drawer locks to prevent climbing.
✓ Remove baking tools from reachable drawers.
✓ Lock the water and ice dispensers on your refrigerator.

✓ Move open and glass containers out of your refrigerator door.
✓ Keep plenty of kid-friendly cabinets.

The Living or Family Room

✓ Secure bookcases to the wall.
✓ Empty low shelves.
✓ Use Plexiglas to protect low shelves.
✓ Secure your television.
✓ Velcro or buy a holder for your remotes.
✓ Lock your fireplace.
✓ Remove glass-topped coffee tables.
✓ Watch for unstable lamps.
✓ Watch for small lamps where the bulb is accessible.

The Bedrooms

✓ Lock your bifold doors.
✓ Police the kids when they're bed jumping.
✓ Drape a towel at the top of the door.
✓ Remove doors.
✓ Use strong curtain rods.
✓ Install curtain tiebacks high up.

The Bathroom

✓ Hide your good makeup.
✓ Put away extra toilet paper.
✓ Keep blow-dryers, hair spray, and contact lens solution out of reach.
✓ Secure shower curtain rods.

Your Home Office

✓ Place your keyboard far back on your desk.
✓ Don't keep loose objects near your computer.
✓ Put away office supplies.
✓ Cover your power strips.

The Area Around the Stairs

✓ Buy gates that screw in.
✓ Watch for sharp edges on gates.
✓ Check pet stores for gates.
✓ Tape your loose rugs.
✓ Teach your twins to go down the stairs.
✓ Affix rubber stair treads.

Outside Your Home
✓ Install a driveway gate.

✓ Drape towels on deck furniture.

✓ Use Plexiglas to secure the railing on your back deck or balcony.

Additional Suggestions
✓ Keep doors to out-of-bounds areas closed.

✓ Install door hooks.

✓ Hang most photos.

✓ Keep watch, don't get distracted.

✓ Have distractions ready for the kids.

✓ Be responsive to new changes.

✓ Create a "safe" zone.

✓ Keep a cordless phone handy.

✓ Put away adult shoes.

✓ Keep extra door locks and heavy-duty ties on hand.

✓ Use hair elastics to secure cabinet doors.

✓ Lock your windows.

✓ Keep your pet dishes covered or out of reach.

✓ Use duct tape on doors with handle locks.

✓ Keep a dustpan and dust brush handy.

✓ Tape a list of emergency numbers on your medicine cabinet.

✓ Buy a Magic Eraser.

✓ Keep extra keys handy.

✓ Mark your keys.

THE FUNDAMENTALS

There are some basic actions that should be taken to make your home safe for your twins.

Deal with the Basics First
Basic baby-proofing includes covering electrical outlets with safety plugs that cap the outlets to make them inaccessible to young children; installing oven and stove-top knob covers; securing window cords; and installing cabinet locks, door handle covers, and toilet locks. Baby gates should also be put up around stairs, and dangerous substances and medications should be removed from where a baby can get to them (such as below the sink). Any credible baby-proofing article or book will offer more detail as to how to implement these steps, and if you really need help, there are numerous baby- or child-

proofing professionals (look online or in a phone book) who can assist you in preparing your home.

THE KITCHEN

The kitchen is a hotbed of potential trouble spots. Cabinets, appliances, sharp implements, and hazardous liquids are all too often within easy reach of young children, and twins may work together to overcome pretty significant obstacles, such as picking up heavy objects. Take extra steps to baby-proof your kitchen.

Double Up on Door Locks

Some children are very adept at opening childproof locks. If your twins fall into this category, install two different types of locks on cabinets so that if one proves vulnerable, the other might hold longer.

Use a Combination Lock If Necessary

Most people know to keep harmful substances like bleach, toilet bowl and window cleaners, dishwashing detergent, and jewelry cleaner out of reach of small children, either by storing those products on high, inaccessible shelves or by locking them up. But childproof locks may not stand a chance against a couple of inquisitive toddlers. If you need to keep harmful substances stored at floor level, such as under a kitchen or bathroom sink, consider using a combination lock (the kind you may have used in high school on your locker) instead of the plastic locks commonly used for childproofing.

Buy Low Stools

If possible, avoid using two-step stools in your kitchen or bath and use low stools instead. Most kids will push and tug at each other to get up onto the stool, and a taller two-step stool simply increases the likelihood that one of your twins will be pulled off and fall onto the floor from a higher distance.

Install Extra Drawer Locks to Prevent Climbing

If you think only the kitchen drawers with sharp or dangerous objects need to be locked, you're dead wrong. One day we found our twins using the drawer pulls as footholds as they tried to climb up to sit on the counter. The problem is that kitchen cabinet drawers are vertically aligned, so the drawer pulls form a little ladder and the drawers themselves open smoothly and silently, so they're easy for the kids to open and tough for us to hear if they are out of our sight line. The top drawers are just about forehead or eyeball height for our three-year-olds, and we've had a couple of close calls where one child has opened a drawer and the other, in a rush to join her brother, has nearly gashed her head on the drawer's sharp corner. The drawers are also perfect for getting fingers slammed inside. Install extra door locks to keep drawers from becoming a climbing wall.

Remove Baking Tools from Reachable Drawers

Knives and forks are not the only kitchen items that are potentially danger-ous if kept in cabinets or drawers. So are rolling pins, potato mashers, meat tenderizers, and whisk attachments for hand mixers. Both rolling pins and hammer-style meat tenderizers are heavy, so if your child picks them up and drops them, she—or her brother—could end up with bruised (or worse) fingers and toes. Potato mashers and whisk attachments are fun until some-one gets bonked over the head with them. Remove these items from reach-able drawers, but leave some other fun baking items like plastic spatulas and wooden spoons so that your twins can still "help out" or at least play kitchen.

Lock the Water and Ice Dispensers on Your Refrigerator

Water and ice dispensers are a huge draw for small children. But unless you want a pretty constant flood of melting ice or streams of water in your kitchen, be sure to disable the dispensers on your fridge.

Move Open and Glass Containers Out of Your Refrigerator Door

Twins will cooperate with each other when it helps them do things they might not be able to accomplish on their own. Opening refrigerator doors is a favorite twin activity you might not think about. Remove any glass or heavy or open containers from inside the refrigerator door. You might think that the heavier an item is, the less likely your twins are to pick it up, but it seems to have just the opposite effect: It makes them more likely to test their strength. Put all things breakable and spillable on the top shelf or way back on a shelf where your twins can't get to them.

Keep Plenty of Kid-Friendly Cabinets

The best way to prevent your twins from getting into things and places they shouldn't is to provide them with plenty of things and places they can get into. Keep several floor-level kitchen cabinets filled with plastic containers, baking pans, and cookie sheets and give the kids free access to open them and rummage around. They'll be less likely to reach for out-of-bounds areas when they're busy helping you in the kitchen. We store their plates and cups, straws, plastic containers, phone books, pots and pans, wooden spoons, spatulas, and measuring spoons in our lower-level cabinets and our twins can make a mess if they wish. The only things we learned not to store there were our extra canned goods. Not such a good idea when the cans are rolling around on the floor or hit someone's toe (okay, mine).

THE LIVING OR FAMILY ROOM

The areas where your family spends most of its time deserve a thorough check. Take special precautions to secure furniture if your twins are climbers.

Secure Bookcases to the Wall
Bookcases are magnets for climbers, but even tall, heavy bookcases may not withstand the weight of two small children climbing together. Make sure to anchor bookshelves to the wall.

Empty Low Shelves
Remove photos, books, knickknacks, and anything else that can get trashed from low shelves. These items will only entice your children to reach out and grab them, and even if they're not grabbers, your twins are very likely to knock them over as they're playing with something else.

Use Plexiglas to Protect Low Shelves
Let's say you can't remove items from child-accessible shelves for space or personal reasons. You can protect those items by covering the shelves with some clear Plexiglas. Go to a hardware store and buy some quarter-inch Plexiglas (be sure to have the dimensions of your bookshelf with you) and have the staff put in a couple of screw holes for you. Then, at home, simply screw in the Plexiglas to cover the lower shelves. When you want to remove it from your bookcase shelf, all you have to do is fill in the holes with some wood filler and sand and stain the wood to match. If you're not that handy, you can also thread heavy-duty ties or some wire in the holes of the Plexiglas and tie the plastic sheet around the bookshelf, tying it shut in the back, where your twins can't get to it.

Secure Your Television
If you think a big, heavy television can't be knocked over by a small child, you're wrong. Our television's plastic casing was all cracked and buckled after our four-year-old daughter pushed it over from the substantial TV shelf it sat on while she was playing with the twins. Needless to add, it cost quite a bit to replace. We're just thankful that the television fell backward and not forward, onto our children.

Velcro or Buy a Holder for Your Remotes

Kids and remotes do not mix. Not only can a remote become easily lost, it can also become a projectile that flies into your television screen, or the battery cover comes loose and it spills batteries on the floor. Invest in a remote holder that you can keep beyond the reach of your twins. Or, conversely, take a lesson from some hospitals and hotels and affix some Velcro to the back of the remotes and to the top of the TV so that you can keep remotes out of your twins' hands but still be able to locate them when needed.

Lock Your Fireplace

A fireplace is at perfect crawling level for a baby and the ideal size for a little one to fit in when trying to play hide-and-seek. Buy and secure in place a screen to make the fireplace off-limits, or install glass doors and make sure to lock them so your twins can't open them. Similarly, remove andirons or other fireplace tools unless you're actually using the fireplace at that moment.

Remove Glass-Topped Coffee Tables

Forget the fancy or gorgeous furniture you had before you had twins. You need utilitarian, who-cares-if-someone-spills-something-or-writes-in-crayon tables and chairs. Glass coffee tables are a particular hazard. Do yourself a favor and temporarily replace the glass top either with Plexiglas or a piece of wood cut to size. To improve its appearance, cover the wood with some batting (to soften it) and fabric before placing it back in the table frame.

Watch for Unstable Lamps

Small children can easily pull down table lamps by tugging on cords. Either secure unstable lamps or remove them entirely.

Watch for Small Lamps Where the Bulb Is Accessible

A hot bulb can easily burn your child, and many small lamps have shades that expose the top part of the bulb. If your kids can reach it while standing on a sofa, chair, or stool, replace the lamp with something safer.

THE BEDROOMS

Bedrooms are pretty safe, except for the door slamming, bed jumping, and curtain pulling, but there are still things your children can get into that should be baby-proofed.

Lock Your Bifold Doors

Many homes have bifold doors, especially for bedroom closets. If your twins' room has bifold doors, I recommend you get a special lock and affix it to the top. Our twins and their sister love to play hide-and-seek in the closet, and we were constantly worried that they'd catch their fingers in the door as it folded or, conversely, that they would destroy the door with their rambunctious play. These locks are pretty easy to find, especially on the Internet. Safety 1st makes a lock for bifold doors, as do a couple of other companies.

Police the Kids When They're Bed Jumping

All children love to jump on beds and sofas, and if you have twins, or twins and another child, you are guaranteed to have frequent bed jumping jamborees in your house because one child will start and the others will follow. And if your house is anything like ours, your bed is likely to be quite high off the ground, with lots of sharp corners from dressers and side tables very close by. This leads to a disaster waiting to happen since it's almost impossible to prevent a child from climbing up and jumping if you're busy taking care of his sisters or brothers. In our house, we chose to police bed jumping in a couple of ways: We allow it in short spurts under our strict supervision on the theory that these sessions will help get it out of their system, and we let the twins jump on their sister's bed, which is much lower to the ground and happens to be in a carpeted room. On vacation, if the bed is fairly low, we surround it with pillows and let the kids go wild for about ten minutes while we stand close by. Other parents say they strictly forbid jumping on the bed, but frankly, in our family, prohibitions have not worked at all—the twins just ignore us or sneak up to our room when we're not there—so we learned to roll with it and manage it instead. Frequently, we'll allow jumping as long as we're right by the bed, but we've also made a habit of turning on the stereo in the bedroom and encouraging the kids to join the "dance party" on the floor, which is just as enticing as jumping on the bed and a lot safer.

Drape a Towel at the Top of the Door

Door slamming becomes an issue as soon as kids can walk, it seems. And the older your twins get, the more likely they are to slam doors to keep their brother or sister out of the room. An easy way to discourage door slamming is to drape a towel over the top of the door.

Remove Doors

If door slamming gets really bad, either because of the noise or because one of your twins has been hurt after getting a hand caught in the door, don't be afraid to remove the door itself, even if it's only for a few days. This is an extremely effective way of communicating your point that slamming doors will not be tolerated.

Use Strong Curtain Rods

In addition to securing window cords (part of basic baby-proofing), test your curtain rods to see how well they can withstand pulling and tugging. Our twins love to play hide-and-seek behind the curtains and have put our curtain rods to the test.

Install Curtain Tiebacks High Up

Tiebacks are drapery hardware that hold curtains away from the window. They are usually installed above the window sill, or roughly at an adult's waist level. The design of the tiebacks means that they jut away from the wall at about the height of your toddler's head. If you have them, install or move the tiebacks high enough so that your twins won't run into them.

THE BATHROOM

Baby-proofing your bathroom involves more than using toilet locks (although those are great). Remove items that will attract kids.

Hide Your Good Makeup

Nothing is more frustrating than seeing little handprints of foundation on your walls. It does not wash off easily and you'll probably have to repaint. The same goes for lipstick, eye shadow, and mascara. Any makeup container that can be opened will be. The makeup will end up all over your twins' clothes, faces, and your walls and floor, and what's worse, you will be out a lot of money as you try and replace that $30 lipstick and $25 foundation. Do yourself a favor and hide the good makeup that you wear everyday and replace it with some innocuous and nonstaining items, like some face puffs or lip gloss that your little ones can use if they want to be just like mom.

Put Away Extra Toilet Paper

It's fascinating to watch a roll of toilet paper unspool; just ask any toddler. And if one child has a piece of toilet paper, the other wants one, too. Before you know it, they're both grabbing at it and there's toilet paper either all over the floor or stuffed inside your toilet. Remove extra rolls for your own peace of mind.

Keep Blow-Dryers, Hair Spray, and Contact Lens Solution Out of Reach

Since you may use blow-dryers, hair spray, and contact lens solution every day, you probably want to keep them handy. Just make sure they're not too handy for your kids. Keep these items on a shelf high enough that they can't be reached by a child on a stool, or better yet, keep them entirely out of sight (hidden in your clothes closet, for example, if it happens to be close to your bathroom).

Secure Shower Curtain Rods

A favorite hiding place in our house is the bathtub, with the shower curtain pulled so that no one can see you. But not only is the tub a hard, slippery surface, the shower curtain rod also poses a danger if it's too flimsy. Consider replacing your spring-mounted shower curtain rod with one that's screwed in. That way, a child who clutches onto a shower curtain to stop herself from slipping won't fall because the shower curtain rod collapses.

YOUR HOME OFFICE

The home office may be your sanctuary, but there are hazards there too, both to your children and to your computer.

Place Your Keyboard Far Back on Your Desk

Discourage your toddlers from climbing up onto your desk and playing with your computer by keeping the keyboard far back beyond their reach. Or you can always keep it disconnected so that even if they play with the keys, your twins won't do something disastrous to your computer files.

Don't Keep Loose Objects Near Your Computer

Loose objects like paper clip holders and paperweights can be picked up and thrown, which means that your monitor, or even one of your children, could get hit. Keep such objects away from your computer.

Put Away Office Supplies

Hide your staplers, scissors, stapler removers, letter opener, and anything else that's sharp.

Cover Your Power Strips

When covering your electrical outlets, don't forget the power strips in your house. Safety 1st makes a special cover that encloses the entire power strip and protects little hands. Go a step further and place the power strip behind your furniture so it's less accessible to your children.

THE AREA AROUND THE STAIRS

Stairs are probably the biggest point of anxiety for new parents and should be secured both from the bottom and the top. Invest extra time and money to make sure your twins are safe in the areas around the stairs in your house.

Buy Gates That Screw In

Protect your children from falling down the stairs by installing the most secure gates possible, the kind that screw in rather than pressure-mounted gates. Be sure to put gates both at the top and the bottom of the stairs, and use them to block off areas you don't want the kids to go in, such as a kitchen or laundry room.

Watch for Sharp Edges on Gates

The hallways in some multiple-level homes can be pretty narrow, and if you've installed a gate at the top of the landing, the clearance may be pretty tight. Pay close attention to your baby gate when opening and closing, especially if it has sharp points extending from the locking mechanism, since the locking mechanism happens to be at roughly the same height as a toddler's head.

Check Pet Stores for Gates

If you can't find a gate that fits your needs (extra-wide doorways, extra-tall gates) in the baby store, try going to a pet store, which may have a larger selection of gates.

Tape Your Loose Rugs

Make sure to secure loose rugs with carpet tape, especially in hallways where you may have carpet runners. Loose rugs can slip, slide, and bunch up, and a toddler can easily end up falling or, worse, falling down the stairs because she was tripped up by a rug.

Teach Your Twins to Go Down the Stairs

Probably the best thing you can do to encourage stair safety in your house is to teach your toddlers to go up and down the stairs themselves. That's not to say you should encourage unsupervised stair climbing, but if one of your twins does get on the stairs, it's important that he know how to get down.

One of our twins was able to crawl up and descend the stairs at about eight months. She crawled up going forward but came down crawling backward— legs first, head last. Her brother was closer to eleven months when he started, but by thirteen or fourteen months, they were both pros. We kept gates up at the bottom and the top of the stairs until the twins were at least eighteen months old, but we let them crawl up the stairs instead of carrying them.

Affix Rubber Stair Treads

If your stairs are slippery, consider affixing rubber stair treads, or at least a carpet, to prevent slipping.

OUTSIDE YOUR HOME

Danger lurks outside your home as well as inside. Take extra measures to protect your twins against unsecured driveways, overheated deck furniture, and unsafe deck railings.

Install a Driveway Gate

If you have a driveway, make sure you invest in a gate to keep your twins from running out into the street. It's particularly difficult to keep an eye on two small children, one of whom may need to be picked up because he's crying while the other is headed for the hills. If you can't or don't want to install a permanent gate, one short-term solution is a retractable mesh gate. The only problem is that mesh gates tend to sag in the middle, and once your twins are big enough they can push the mesh fabric up and climb under, or push it down and climb over. But these gates are definitely worth it if you need a quick and short-term fix.

Drape Towels on Deck Furniture

Help prevent your children from getting their fingers pinched or from burning themselves on hot plastic or metal deck furniture by draping towels over chairs and chaise longues.

Use Plexiglas to Secure the Railing on Your Back Deck or Balcony

If the rails on your deck or balcony are widely spaced, or there's a piece that your twins can step on to climb the railing, you may want to consider securing some sheets of Plexiglas to them. It's a nice solution because the Plexiglas is see-through, so it won't block the view, but it will protect your toddlers from climbing or getting stuck between the rails.

ADDITIONAL SUGGESTIONS

There are plenty of other tricks you can use to make your home an overall safer environment, from hanging photos instead of displaying them on shelves to creating a safe zone for your twins.

Keep Doors to Out-of-Bounds Areas Closed

If you don't want your twins to go somewhere, a good first barrier is to simply keep the door closed.

Install Door Hooks

For rooms that are off-limits, install door hooks and mount them at the top, where your twins can't reach them even if standing on a stool or chair. Remove them as soon as your child figures out how to open them.

Hang Most Photos

Look around, and if you have a lot of photos on your tables and shelves, consider removing them. Otherwise, you may have to deal with broken glass and cuts. Hang photos on the wall instead.

Keep Watch, Don't Get Distracted

If you've done a good job preparing your home for safety, it's easy to get a little lax in terms of watching your twins. But the simple fact that there are two babies means you cannot take anything for granted—even as you're watching one, the other twin can be getting into trouble. Avoid distractions and keep an eagle eye on both children.

Have Distractions Ready for the Kids

Baby-proofing can backfire if too much stuff is off-limits to your twins. Prepare some distractions to keep their attention instead. An extra laundry basket in the bedroom can easily become a pretend boat, which has the added bonus of keeping them out of the closet you don't want them in.

Be Responsive to New Changes

As your twins grow, so too will the things they're interested in, and a baby who showed no interest in pulling up plants suddenly starts eating them at every opportunity. Pay attention to what your twins do and adjust your baby-proofing actions accordingly.

Create a "Safe" Zone

Create at least one area in your house that is completely baby-proof in case you have to leave one child or both of them for a moment or two. The safe zone can be as small as a Pack 'n Play or as large as a cordoned-off room.

Keep a Cordless Phone Handy

Invest in a phone with multiple cordless handsets. You'll always be close to a phone in case of emergency and, if you're giving your twins a bath, you can take it into the bathroom with you.

Put Away Adult Shoes

This may sound silly, but put away your shoes so that your twins aren't tempted to wear them. Toddlers love to try on your shoes, but if they put them on and start walking in them while you're not there, they can easily trip and fall down the stairs.

Keep Extra Door Locks and Heavy-Duty Ties on Hand

Unfortunately, some childproof locks break pretty easily or get lost when you constantly have to put them on and take them off. Keep a stash of extras just in case.

Use Hair Elastics to Secure Cabinet Doors

Some cabinets securely perfectly well with a hair elastic, especially two-door cabinets with knobs that are side-by-side. Avoid using regular rubber bands for an extended period of time, because the rubber can thin and wear away.

Lock Your Windows

If your windows are low to the ground or within reaching distance of your twins, make sure they lock so that the window can only be pushed up or out to a certain point. Some windows have automatic locks that only allow you to open them six inches or so. For other windows, you can install hook and chain locks to prevent them from opening outward beyond a certain point, or cover the bottom portion with Plexiglas so that while you can still open the window to let in fresh air, the space is blocked off to your babies. Window guards, which are usually made of metal bars, are also another good option. Guardian Angel is one well-known brand that offers window guards for many different types of windows.

Keep Your Pet Dishes Covered or Out of Reach

If you have pets, put away their food and water dishes unless you want to find your twins with a mouthful of cat or dog food. Feed your pets only at a time of day when you can supervise, or buy automatic feeding and water bowls (which only fill the bowls with predetermined portions at preset times), or put the food bowls completely out of reach of your twins—behind a screened partition, for example.

Use Duct Tape on Doors with Handle Locks
Disable door handle locks by covering the knobs with duct tape.

Keep a Dustpan and Dust Brush Handy
It doesn't matter how much baby-proofing you do, there are plenty of occasions where your twins break or spill something. Keep extra dustpans and brushes handy in various rooms of your house. Then, if there is a reason you need to clean up, you don't have to leave the room or leave the mess within reach of your babies.

Tape a List of Emergency Numbers on Your Medicine Cabinet
Type up a list of emergency phone numbers, including poison control, your pediatrician, pharmacy, and family contacts, and keep it taped on the inside of your medicine cabinet door. This way, not only is it in a designated place in your house, it's also close to your twins' prescriptions should you need to refer to the package.

Buy a Magic Eraser
Technically not a baby-proofing item, a Magic Eraser will make your life with twins much easier. It's great for cleaning off crayon, smudges, and other marks on your walls. Get a few packs, because you will definitely go through them.

Keep Extra Keys Handy
If you have rooms with locks, keep extra keys handy in a safe place (but not in the room that locks, of course). Case in point: The door to our home office locks and one day our twins got themselves locked inside. They were safe in the house, but alone in the office where we couldn't get in. It took us several minutes to hunt down the keys to the door—and those were several minutes of sheer panic.

Mark Your Keys
Okay, you have lots of keys to lots of locks, but when you need them in an emergency, you can't figure out which is which. Mark your keys with color-coded covers, or even stickers, so you can recognize and find them quickly.

17

The Best Life-with-Twins Tips Ever

After all is said and done, and you've subdivided your day into small, discrete, *manageable* categories to accommodate your new life with twins, there are still huge swaths of time and enormous responsibilities that seem unmanageable. Parents of twins need to be simultaneously organized and easygoing. They need to take care of themselves even as they take care of their babies. And they should take advantage of every shortcut, trick, and strategy other parents of twins have discovered and have shared here. What follows is advice on things big and small that only a parent who has been there before can attest to. Good luck!

Making Life Easier for Yourself
✓ Schedule, schedule, schedule.
✓ Go with the flow.
✓ Take as many naps as possible.
✓ Baby your back.
✓ Don't worry if you can't tell your twins apart.
✓ Go ahead and cry.
✓ Ask for support, but not always from the same person.
✓ Get a mother's helper.
✓ Release tension and frustration.

Making Life Easier for Your Twins
✓ Call them by their names.
✓ Research early intervention programs.

✓ Separate your twins in school.
✓ Spend time alone with each twin.

More Ways to Organize Your Life

✓ Create a custom baby-care schedule.
✓ Create two medicine kits, one for each baby.
✓ Organize your outdoor items and keep them near the door.
✓ Splurge on a cleaning lady.
✓ Schedule all healthcare appointments for the same day.

Additional Tips for Making Your Life with Twins Easier

✓ Buy a white-noise machine.
✓ Use Podee bottles in the car.
✓ Buy a couple of Step2 Push-Around Buggies.
✓ Create your own take-along activity box.
✓ Get a copy of *1-2-3 Magic: Effective Discipline for Children 2–12* from the bookstore.
✓ Use rubber mats on hardwood floors.
✓ Use regular laundry detergent.
✓ Have a photographer come to your home.
✓ Entertain yourselves at home.
✓ Cook at night or in the morning.
✓ Have family members babysit in pairs.
✓ Bring along a mom when shopping for baby items.
✓ Get two memento boxes.
✓ Create online photo albums.
✓ Get triple prints of photos.
✓ Take advantage of multiples discounts.
✓ Shop at stores that cater to teachers or preschools.
✓ Take photos, because time goes fast!

MAKING LIFE EASIER FOR YOURSELF

There are plenty of things you can do to make your life with twins a bit easier, from creating a schedule and letting go of unrealistic expectations, to finding outlets for yourself to get some rest and support and release stress.

Schedule, Schedule, Schedule

If organization was not your strong suit before you became pregnant with twins, it may very well be after they are born. Becoming organized will be your biggest "secret weapon" to successful parenting. This means putting your babies on a schedule as far as feedings and naps go, as well as organizing your backpack or diaper bags (or both), your car, and your house. Since everything takes so much longer to accomplish when there are two babies to care for, knowing where everything is and doing tasks at certain specific times of the day will help you manage the chaos. You don't have to become a slave to your schedule, but it does help to keep things on track.

Go with the Flow

Taking care of twins is like being carried off by a great wave—you're not sure what's happening, you're just trying to keep your head above water. Most mothers of multiples say that flexibility is critical, as is dropping the ideal of having a spotless home and home-cooked meals every day and night. If you're trying to parent twins, let go of your idea of perfection. It doesn't matter if the house is messy or your laundry's not done and you're making microwave meals for dinner. In the long run, none of that matters. What matters is that your twins and your family are healthy and whole.

Take as Many Naps as Possible

Yes, you hear this bit of advice all the time, but for parents of twins it will have special resonance. With two babies, you may only be sleeping for one-and-a-half or two-hour stretches at a time in between all the feedings. Ignore the mess in your home and instead invest in yourself by sleeping whenever the babies do. My husband and I took regular naps until the babies were at least three months old. If a family member came over, one of us might visit with them while the other slept, or sometimes we would both only visit for fifteen minutes, then we'd both leave and take naps. Everyone understood.

Baby Your Back

It's pretty easy to carry both babies at the same time once you get the hang of it, but after a while the weight of your twins can really be a drag. Nonetheless, they will still tug and pull to be picked up. Avoid back problems by stretching routinely (ideally every day) and remember to lift with your knees, not with your back, especially when you're trying to pick up and hold two thirty-pound preschoolers.

Don't Worry If You Can't Tell Your Twins Apart

As one mother of twins told me, you don't get some mythical gift that allows you to tell your identical twins apart. You can often see subtle differences between them if they are lying side-by-side, but it may be hard to tell who's who, especially if you're only looking at one baby or if both babies are bundled up. Some simple ways to tell twins apart include dabbing nail polish on the toenail of one baby, having your babies wear ID bracelets (they don't have to be hospital bracelets, but those work, too), or dressing them in different colors.

Go Ahead and Cry

Yes, you will feel like it, many, many times and for many, many reasons. Give in and let it out for a while until you feel better and can focus again.

Ask for Support, but Not Always from the Same Person

You will certainly need support from your friends and family, but try and parcel out your problems among several of them. Try not to vent to the same person. You don't want him or her to become burned out listening to you and your problems, and you also don't want to get a reputation as a whiner or as someone who constantly needs help.

Get a Mother's Helper

You may not be able to afford a nanny or a regular babysitter, but you can probably find a responsible teenager to come help you out after school. Contact the principal or guidance counselor at your local high school, or contact your place of worship for names and recommendations if you don't already know someone you can call on.

Release Tension and Frustration

Beat up a pillow, go for a walk, or if you're really ambitious, go for a jog. Parenting twins is very difficult, and with the near-constant sleep deprivation, you will often find yourself ready to snap. It's important to do something for yourself to help you relax, to give you energy, and to keep you from fighting over stupid things with your equally tired and frustrated spouse.

MAKING LIFE EASIER FOR YOUR TWINS

If your twins have special needs, there are a lot of resources you can tap. But one of the most important things you can do for your twins is to treat them as individuals, not as two parts of a unit.

Call Them by Their Names

It's so easy to get into the habit of calling them "the twins" or "the babies," but it's important to refer to children by their given names so they develop a sense that you value them as individuals.

Research Early Intervention Programs

If your twins were born prematurely, they could very well be eligible for early intervention programs that provide in-home visits, family counseling, speech therapy, and physical occupational therapy, among other services. Many programs are part of the Children with Special Health Care Needs provision of the Social Security Act and may have different names depending on the state where you live. Contact your state health department for more information, or do an online search for "children with special health needs."

Separate Your Twins in School

If possible, separate your twins when they enter kindergarten or first grade so they have an opportunity to form their own friendships and, in turn, be treated as special and unique individuals rather than as part of a package. If your twins are in preschool or day care, consider sending them each separately for at least one day a week to help them learn to socialize with children besides their twin.

Spend Time Alone with Each Twin

Admittedly, spending time alone with each twin can be hard to do, especially when they are babies. If you need to go somewhere, they're both with you; if you are home, they're both with you. But as your children grow and you get more adept at carrying out their routines (sleeping, feedings, baths), try and take only one baby with you on any given errand while your spouse or another family member watches the other baby. It can be as little as thirty minutes, once a week, but it does make a difference by giving you an opportunity to spend alone time and build rapport with that child as an individual.

MORE WAYS TO ORGANIZE YOUR LIFE

Parents of twins find their own shortcuts to getting things done. Here are some great ideas that can help you get more organized.

Create a Custom Baby-Care Schedule

When your twins are babies, you'll be tracking their every feeding, including how many bottles they drink, their every diaper change, and even their naps and sleep schedule. To make this process easier, prepare some blank sheets with categories for feedings, diaper changes, and sleep; create a column for each baby as well. Keep the sheets on your refrigerator door with a magnet and either jot down details for each baby or simply check off items as they're done. This sheet will come in especially handy if you and your spouse are taking shifts. If you're the spouse just beginning your shift, you can just look at the sheet to see what happened while you were asleep.

Create Two Medicine Kits, One for Each Baby

Rather than trying to sift through a jumble of medicines or figure out which aspirator you used on which baby, create separate medicine kits by storing each baby's medicines and supplies in small, clear plastic bins. Label the bins with each baby's name and stock it with some standard over-the-counter medications, such as Tylenol (for pain and fever) and Mylicon drops (for indigestion); a few medicine spoons or syringes; an aspirator; diaper lotion; thermometer; fingernail clippers; and any prescription medicines your twins may use. Keeping these items separate will not only help you find the prescription medicines at a moment's notice, but it will help you track how much medicine each of your children has received. In a pinch, having doubles will also ensure that you don't run out of medicine at the most inopportune moment. Cold medicines are no longer available for children under two, so they won't be part of your medicine kits.

Organize Your Outdoor Items and Keep Them Near the Door

You can either get several clear plastic bins or buy a special toy organizer, the kind that has twelve or so open plastic bins that sit on a three-shelf wooden frame. Use the bins to store outdoor seasonal items like sunglasses and sunblock, hats, gloves, and umbrellas, as well as anything you use in the yard or the car, such as baby rattles, car toys, and even cameras. Don't forget to label the bins and keep them by the door you enter and exit most often.

Splurge on a Cleaning Lady

If you are one of those people who needs to have everything organized, the best thing you can do for yourself is to splurge on a cleaning lady. Do it once a week or every other week if you can afford it. But if you can't, splurge on a cleaning lady once every few months, such as before a holiday or before your twins' first birthday party. Knowing that someone will actually clean the grout in your bathroom, dust the ceiling fans, and mop the floors instead of just wishing you had the time to do it yourself is nirvana! For those who really cannot afford it, ask your friends to chip in and give a housecleaning service as a shower gift.

Schedule All Healthcare Appointments for the Same Day

It's so much easier to take one day off from work to take all of your kids to their various healthcare appointments than it is to take several full or half days off to accompany each child separately. We try to schedule appointments to both the doctor *and* the dentist for all three kids on the same day, so we get everything taken care of in the course of one morning.

ADDITIONAL TIPS FOR MAKING YOUR LIFE WITH TWINS EASIER

Finally, here are some of the everyday pointers that make someone's life with twins a bit easier, and they can help you, too. These tips are truly parent-tested.

Buy a White-Noise Machine

No matter how deeply you normally sleep, you cannot beat a white-noise machine for drowning out disturbing noise, such as two crying babies. These machines are indispensable if you and your spouse take shifts and one of you needs to sleep while the other is taking care of the twins. If your bedroom is in close proximity to your children's bedroom, a noise machine can have a pretty long life in your home, even after you stop taking naps. It works really well if you have to be up earlier or you stay up later than your twins, since it helps drown out any noises that might wake up the babies. Some parents also use noise machines in the twins' room or attached to each crib to help the babies sleep.

Use Podee Bottles in the Car

Podee hands-free baby bottles (discussed in Chapter 9) allow you to feed both babies simultaneously. Even better, they allow you to feed your babies when you're doing other things, like driving or running errands. They'll save both time and your sanity, since you don't have to stop for thirty or forty minutes in the middle of whatever errand you're trying to accomplish to feed your twins or to listen to them shriek because they're hungry while you're driving.

Buy a Couple of Step2 Push-Around Buggies

These plastic buggies (from The Step2 Company) are a great alternative to umbrella strollers, and they are a fantastic way for one adult to push two small children at a time. I can't say enough about how much I love them. Kids think the buggies are fun because they're car-shaped (with a horn) and because they get to sit upright in the car, belted in for safety. The buggies are very lightweight and have long handles, so they're easy to lift and push, and they have a little storage compartment under the car hood that is perfect for a couple of diapers, some drinks, and even a pail and shovel. I bought these buggies on a lark because I thought they were cute and we have used them virtually every single day (even in the winter) for nearly three years. They're really a bargain at about $45 each.

Create Your Own Take-Along Activity Box

Family-friendly restaurants often have paper and crayons that will keep your kids happy, at least for a while. But you can go several steps beyond the five-crayon pack and single sheet of paper typically provided by some restaurants by creating your own activity pack to take along with you to places where your kids will have to wait, such as non-family-friendly restaurants, a dentist's or doctor's office, or your hair salon (if you're forced to take them with you). Buy an inexpensive art or craft bin at the craft store (the kind with a closed lid and a handle) and fill it with markers, crayons, glue sticks, small stickers, and some paper. You can also fit some small toys in the bin, while older kids will enjoy activity and Mad Libs books or magnet-type games. Keep the activity box in your car for those unexpected times when you need to keep your kids quiet.

Get a Copy of *1-2-3 Magic: Effective Discipline for Children 2–12* from the Bookstore

Although it's certainly not the only book available on the topic of discipline, *1-2-3 Magic*, by Thomas W. Phelan, has great word-of-mouth from many parents who have grappled with discipline issues. I happened to hear about the book in passing when my oldest daughter was a toddler. Since then, we have essentially used the same techniques with our twins. Phelan's instructions are very simple and his techniques are truly effective. If you are beside yourself trying to manage your twins, you should at least give Phelan's book a try.

Use Rubber Mats on Hardwood Floors

If you've got hardwood floors and you're worried about safety as your twins are starting to walk, try using interlocking rubber mats to soften their inevitable falls. A friend used these mats in her home, not only to protect her twins, but also to create a more inviting play area in her apartment, since the twins were confined there during the day.

Use Regular Laundry Detergent

Yes, you can buy special laundry detergent just for baby clothes. But it's a waste of time and money to do so if you've got four to six loads of laundry to do every other day. Use the same laundry detergent that you do for your adult clothes and do minimal sorting.

Have a Photographer Come to Your Home

If you ever want to pointlessly waste an entire afternoon, take your babies to a children's photo studio. By the time one twin is ready, the other is melting down. Plus, all of your efforts to get them to smile or even to just stop crying will be fruitless, so your pictures will document two red-faced screaming babies. It may be reality, but not necessarily a reality you will want to remember forever. Instead, get the photographer to come to your home, where everyone is comfortable and you have plenty of changes of clothing.

Entertain Yourselves at Home

If you can afford it, splurge on a TiVo digital video recorder so that you and your spouse or partner can watch programs you want to see during those middle-of-the-night baby shifts, instead of the endless infomercials that run on most channels at 3:00 a.m. Or, get the Wii interactive video game system if you like gaming, or at least sign up for Netflix to get movies delivered to your house. It really helps to provide yourselves with some entertainment options at home, because with two babies to care for, you won't be leaving the house together for quite a while.

Cook at Night or in the Morning

Depending on how you divide baby-care duties with your spouse or partner, you may find yourself wide-awake at 2:00 a.m. or 5:00 a.m. while everyone else is asleep. Take advantage of these lulls to cook dinners in advance to reheat later in the day or to freeze for future meals. My husband had the early-morning shift with the babies, from 2:00 a.m. to 8:00 a.m. (then he'd go to bed around 8:00 p.m.), and he would often prepare Crock-Pot meals in the wee hours while the rest of us slept. He'd peel, chop, and set the dish to cook so that there'd be real food to eat later in the day.

Have Family Members Babysit in Pairs

As a parent of twins, you already know how difficult it is to care for two babies. The rule is pretty much two babies, two adults. If someone in your family (or among your friends, of course) agrees to babysit your twins, see if they can partner up with someone else. It will be less traumatic for grandma or your aunt if she has a helper when babysitting. When our twins were about three months old, our wonderful friend Lisa offered to babysit while we went to a movie, and the poor woman barely got to sit for five minutes! And she was an experienced sitter with nieces who were twins.

Bring Along a Mom When Shopping for Baby Items

If you have a friend who has a young child, or who recently had a baby, ask her to go shopping with you and act as a sounding board and shopping guide. Baby products get constantly updated and there's no one like a new mom to give you the lowdown on things you'll need. The friend doesn't have to be a parent of twins (although that would be ideal), just someone who has recently used or is still using a diaper pail, bouncy chair, car seat, Exersaucer, diaper bag, or other myriad baby things. She'll be able to give you some tips.

Get Two Memento Boxes

Forget about trying to create two baby photo albums. It'll likely never happen, because you'll be too exhausted to actually organize them. Instead get two nice-size and nice-looking boxes, one for each baby, and keep them fairly handy (we keep ours in the twins' closet). Whenever I want to save something, whether a lock of hair, their foot- and handprints, or the outfits they wore coming home from the hospital, I just drop it in the box. Because I have two boxes, I don't have to worry that I'll mix things up, nor do I have the guilty feeling that I'm not doing anything to document their special moments, because the boxes have plenty of mementos in them.

Create Online Photo Albums

You can avoid all of the pressure of having to organize and put together your own photo albums by creating photo albums online. There are plenty of online services, including Shutterfly and PhotoWorks (or if you have a Mac, you can just use the built-in software), that let you create amazing photo albums that can be printed and cloth bound, some with separate book jackets so they look like "real" books. The best part is that you can print only the photos that are really good, and you can make multiple copies of the books for the babies when they grow up or to give to relatives as gifts.

Get Triple Prints of Photos

If you really do want to create photo albums for your twins but choose not to use an online service, then have your photos developed on a regular basis and make sure to get triple prints right there and then. It's a pretty rare parent of twins who has the time and can make the effort to sift through photos and choose which ones to develop in multiples. Just go ahead and do it the first time. At least then you'll have everything on hand if you do ever get around to making the albums.

Take Advantage of Multiples Discounts

A number of companies that sell baby items offer discounts for multiples as long as you provide them with proof, usually a birth certificate. Tiny Love (which makes mobiles and other developmental toys) offers two-for-one items, while Babies "R" Us offers a 10 percent discount when you're buying multiples of the same item. Companies selling diapers (Drypers Corp. and Kimberly-Clark, which makes Huggies), food (Beech-Nut), formula (Carnation/Nestle), bottles (Evenflo), clothes (Healthtex), and toys (Fisher-Price) all offer either discounts or coupons. Usually you have to call the company directly to take part in the discount programs.

Shop at Stores That Cater to Teachers or Preschools

Stores that specialize in educational toys and preschool supplies are a boon to parents of twins and large families. At these stores you'll find oversize wagons that can seat four children (the kind used in preschools) and super-fun learning toys. Two good sources are www.learningresources.com and www.lakeshorelearning.com (which sells the Easy-Ride Jumbo Wagon that our kids love).

Take Photos, Because Time Goes Fast!

Carry a digital camera everywhere and, if you can, buy a video camera, because before you know it, your two-week-old babies are two months old, then two years old, then in grade school. Of course, you'll have gray hair and wrinkles regardless of your actual age just from the stress of raising twins, but won't you be happier with some pictures to remind you of just how amazing it all is, every day?

Appendix: Resources

ORGANIZATIONS

National Organization of Mothers of Twins Clubs (NOMOTC), Inc.

This nonprofit organization is "a support group for parents of twins and higher-order multiples." It's a great umbrella organization, and its website at www.nomotc.org has links to state and local clubs, many of which have their own resource links. For example, click on Illinois, and you'll find twenty local organizations that you can get involved with. Click on New Jersey and you'll find eighteen clubs. NOMTC holds conventions, publishes a journal, collects data on multiples, and maintains a bibliography of twins-related publications. It is an understatement to say that it is thorough in addressing all issues of interest to the parents of multiples.

International Society for Twin Studies

This Australian organization publishes an academic journal, *Twin Research and Human Genetics,* which is available to subscribers. The group's website (www.ists.qimr.edu.au) has information on international twins and multiples organizations, divided by country, including information on health issues and bereavement.

La Leche League International (LLLI)

La Leche League (www.llli.org) is the premier resource for breast-feeding information, with many resources for mothers of twins. Search for "twins" or "multiples" on its website to get links to forums and publications.

Center for the Study of Multiple Birth

This nonprofit organization distributes information on multiples (both twins and higher-order multiples, such as triplets or quadruplets), sponsors scientific conferences, and conducts research related to multiple births. For the nonscientists among us, the group's website (www .multiplebirth.com) offers a robust selection of articles and some interesting statistics on twins and multiples.

WEBSITES/FORUMS

Twinstuff.com

This site is an absolute must for web-savvy parents of twins. The forums, in particular, are extensive and cover virtually every subject under the sun as it relates to twins. The forums are subdivided by age and area of interest, and there are even several forums devoted to topics such as travel, being married to a twin, and the twin bond. Forum members are pretty close-knit (judging by the frequency of their posts), but they are also very helpful to people who just stumble on the site. Definitely worth checking out.

Twinsworld.com

This website is a catchall of commercial (merchandise) and random (jokes, contests, events) twins information. Did you know there is even a restaurant staffed entirely by twins? There are also links to international twins organizations, including organizations in Ghana, Nigeria, Belarus, Sri Lanka, Canada, and South Africa, as well as twin study and support groups.

Twinsonline.co.uk

This U.K.-based site offers a slew of information on parenting twins, as well as a forum and information on research. Although not all of the information is transferable to American users since it features U.K.-based organizations and products, it is helpful nonetheless because it provides proof that parents of twins deal with the same issues regardless of their nationality. A nice counterpart to Twinstuff.com.

Father2Father.com

Resources for fathers of twins are hard to find. Father2Father is an Internet community for fathers of higher-order multiples (triplets and quadruplets, mostly), but dads of twins can find information pertinent to their own situations and get advice and support from fathers around the world. The community is open to members only, so you have to sign up on the site, although there is no cost involved.

ChildrensDisabilities.info

This website provides information on various childhood disabilities, such as attention deficit hyperactivity disorder (ADHD) and cerebral palsy, as well as a page devoted to preemies. The preemies information includes the experiences of parents whose children have been in the neonatal intensive care unit (NICU) and links to parent support groups, among other options.

Prematurity.org

This is a comprehensive website of information for parents of preemies. It has sections on "surviving the NICU," special needs and development, preemie baby stories, preemie research, and parenting the older preemie.

Preemies.org

Another useful site for parents of preemies. Although its selections are more limited, it does offer a chat room and links to resources.

PUBLICATIONS

TWINS Magazine

For everything twins-related, consider a subscription to *TWINS* magazine. The website (www.twinsmagazine.com) also offers an extensive list of books for and about twins, message boards, and an online store for twins-related items.

Baby Bargains

Authors Denise and Alan Fields publish reviews of a wide range of baby products, from strollers to clothing, in their book *Baby Bargains*. Though they don't focus on twins-related products, their reviews are so comprehensive and plainspoken you'll still find the book invaluable as you go shopping for baby gear. Their website (www.WindsorPeak.com) offers updates on product recalls, as well as a blog and message board. The site and book are good resources to get the lowdown on product quality.

SELECTED PRODUCTS AND PROVIDERS

Double Blessings

Double Blessings is a supplier of twin specialty products offered in stores nationwide and online (www.doubleblessings.com). It has a particularly large selection of nursing pillows, including the EZ-2-Nurse Twins pillow, the product that launched the business.

BOB Gear

BOB is an Idaho-based company that makes excellent, high-end walking and jogging strollers, including several models for twins. The BOB Revolution Duallie, for example, features a swiveling front wheel and a lightweight frame and retails for roughly $530. You can find retailers that stock or sell BOB strollers by going to the company's website, www.bobgear.com, or by calling 1-800-893-2447.

Valco Baby

This Australian company offers one of the best solutions for parents of twins and a toddler. You can purchase a toddler seat that attaches to the front of the Valco TriMode twin stroller, so your twins and their older sibling can ride in style. The company even offers a limited-edition pink and blue stroller for boy-girl twins. Check it out at www.valcobaby.com or call 1-800-610-7850.

Go-Go Babyz

This company offers a number of baby products, including the super-handy Kidz Travelmate and Infant Cruizer, travel systems that attach wheels and a handle to your child or infant car seat (fantastic in airports!) More information is available at www.gogobabyz.com or by calling 1-888-686-2552.

Double Snap-N-Go Twin Stroller by Baby Trend

Find this lightweight, collapsible stroller frame at multiple retailers, including Babies "R" Us and Amazon. Product information is available at www.babytrend.com or by calling 1-800-328-7363.

Bedbugz Bed Bolster (by ToddlerCoddler)/Bed Bolster to Go (One Step Ahead)

These inflatable bolster pillows are a great alternative to standard bed rails for toddlers, especially if you are traveling. The bolsters are available from a number of retailers under the Bedbugz brand name. At One Step Ahead stores, the bolster pillows are called "Bed Bolster to Go." Visit www.toddlercoddler.com (1-877-263-3537) for the Bedbugz product and www.onestepahead.com (1-800-950-5120) for the Bed Bolster to Go product.

J.L. Childress

J.L. Childress products include the Wheelie Car Seat Travel Bag. You can get more information about the Wheelie bag or the company's other products either on the company's website, www.jlchildress.com, or by calling 714-939-9376.

Mountain Buggy

Mountain Buggy makes both double and triple strollers. Check out its products on the company's website, www.mountainbuggyusa.com, or by calling 1-866-524-8805

MacLaren

MacLaren makes two styles of strollers for twins: the Twin Triumph and Twin Techno. Get more information about the strollers and the company's other products at www.maclarenbaby.com/us or by calling 1-877-442-4622.

Index